Bourbon & Blues

Hans Offringa

Bourbon & Blues

Conceptual Continuity

© 2011
Hans Offringa
Conceptual Continuity

Photography: Hans Offringa
Design: Becky Offringa
Contributing Editors: Jack McCray, Jim Rutledge

ISBN 978-90-78668-00-8

www.hansoffringa.com
www.thewhiskycouple.com

For Becky

the song of my life

Table of Contents

FOREWORD

Foreword

I first met Hans and Becky Offringa in May 2006 when they were touring Tennessee and Kentucky distilleries. We spent several hours together that day as we discussed Kentucky Bourbon, toured the distillery and tasted a variety of bourbon brands plus bourbon distillates (often referred to as white dog) straight off the still. As we talked it didn't take long for me to realize the passion for bourbon that lived within Hans. Hans, Becky and I established a common bond on that first visit several years ago that ultimately has blossomed into a life long friendship.

Hans honored me with an autographed copy of his *Whisky & Jazz* book a couple years ago. As I read his book I further realized the breadth of his knowledge and passion for all whiskies of the world. His writing style and the ability to interlace the art of music with the art of distilling whisky was so captivating I was unable to put the book down until it was finished, and as I finished I found myself wishing there was more to read. I thought, wouldn't it be wonderful if he would tell the story of bourbon in similar fashion. When I spoke to him about the idea I was not surprised to hear that he and Becky had begun their research on "The Blues" style of music – for a book on bourbon whiskey. They had completed their studies of bourbon and their library of distillery photographs was more then ample. I was intrigued with the perception that the blues and bourbon could somehow be woven together equally as artfully as he had accomplished with *Whiskey & Jazz*. Bourbon and Blues - what could be the connection?

Thinking back on the history of America to the time the new country began its movement to the western frontiers in the mid 18th century many families settled and established residency in areas that would eventually become the states of Tennessee and Kentucky. One of the incentives to move west was land grants offered to families that established footholds on lands of the western frontier territories, grew crops of grain for one year, and if they survived the year the land would become their personal property. Many of the farmers were distillers and brought their stills with them on the difficult and often perilous journey west. They knew it was easier to store their crops of grain in barrels of liquid – distilled spirits - and the distilled spirits could also be used for trade, barter and a degree of pleasure and relaxation from the toils of their labor, and eventually spirits would become a legitimate source of revenue. The primary trading port for their spirits (which was also used for medicinal purpose to cure many of their ills – real or perceived) was New Orleans in the early years. The farmers would load barrels of bourbon on their rafts and float down the Ohio, Tennessee and other rivers to the Mississippi River and then onto New Orleans.

Slavery, often referred to as "the national shame," was abolished in the southern states in the 1860s as consequence of the Civil War between the northern and southern states. Although the slaves were freed of ownership there was very little freedom for the African-Americans –

especially in the early years following the Civil War and the Emancipation Proclamation issued by President Abraham Lincoln. From dawn to dusk the former slaves labored on farms and plantations for a pittance of wage, or as share-croppers. Sunday was a day of rest and on Saturday evenings many would gather at plantations for house parties and fish fries for inexpensive entertainment and sing their field songs, which were filled with "the blues" for the many years of struggle and strife they had endured. One of the hotbeds and birth places of the blues was the Mississippi Delta – which lies between Memphis, Tennessee and Jackson, Mississippi – and was often a stopping off place for the farmers' as they floated their rafts loaded with barrels of bourbon down the Mississippi River. Thus the first ties of Bourbon and Blues.

Hans begins his masterpiece with a brief history of bourbon followed by a history of Blues music, which he takes back to the years of slave ships. He melds a bourbon distillery of today with a blues musician and in so doing tells the history of bourbon and the artistry of the bourbon making process in an entertaining manner never before seen in print. He has published a book that bourbon enthusiasts and connoisseurs as well as novices to the world of beverage alcohols will most certainly enjoy. After reading the first page it will be difficult for a reader to lay the book down before the last word has been absorbed.

Famed Blues musician Dexter Gordon once said, "You gotta have heart if you to want to make it in this business." That is true for the passion and art found in bourbon distillers as well as the blues singers. B.B. King was quoted, "The beautiful thing about learning is nobody can take it away from you." Hans illustrates the passion in his heart for bourbon whiskey and makes learning an entertaining joy.

Jim Rutledge
Master Distiller Four Roses

INTRO

Duality

For more than 30 years I have been a professional writer. I started as a proofreader at a Dutch publishing company in 1974 to earn money for my study in English Literature, which I pursued in evening school. The publisher soon found out I could write because I showed him early scribblings as an editor for my high school newspaper. He offered me a job as an editor and part-time author for his special interest magazines. I learned to love research from that job. Eight years later I left the publisher to work for an advertising agency as a copywriter. In 1984 I established myself as an independent media consultant and writer. To date I have written three novels, a couple of historical books, four illustrated books and many, many publications and books about whisky and whiskey, a drink I became acquainted with when graduating from high school. I immediately loved it. Over time I became what people like to refer to as a whisky connoisseur, but I consider myself first and foremost a writer - notwithstanding the fact that whisky is an important part of my work.

Blues came into my life at age 13, when I purchased the 1969 album *Led Zeppelin II* and heard "Killing Floor" (aka "The Lemon Song"). During high school I played bass in a hard rock band, but that only lasted two years. I got a job and sold my bass for a few bottles of whisky. Then, at the age of 23 I met an amazing guy who became a close friend and still is, Klaas Vermeulen. He plays such a mean blues harp that he was invited to play at the North Sea Jazz Festival and jammed backstage with Sugar Blue way back in the early 1980s. He introduced me to the rich world of blues and together we went to many concerts, seeing Willie Dixon, Albert Collins, Sonny Terry and Brownie Mc-Gee, Hammie Nixon and Sleepy John Estes, R.L. Burnside, Buddy Guy, B.B. King, Johnny Copeland, Big Walter Horton and John Lee Hooker. It finally dawned upon me where Led Zeppelin got their material.

Klaas subsequently joined a then-famous Dutch blues band for which I became a sound and light technician (and a not too successful booking agent). I managed a double life for three years, but being on the road took its toll. Becoming ambivalent about either staying in the music world or focusing on full time writing, I chose the latter. My blues buddy continued playing evening gigs while working full time at an insurance company. We started to explore the world of jazz and saw the likes of Miles Davis, among many other artists. I learned to love jazz and discovered it was deeply rooted in the blues.

From the mid 1990s onward I made trips to the USA yearly, doing consulting work for a media company. These trips took me to Las Vegas, San Francisco and Los Angeles where I frequented B.B. King's Blues Club and saw a young Eric Sardinas perform. In 2001 I broadened my horizon and got a consulting job in Charleston, SC, where I discovered a very lively jazz and blues scene. I not only fell in love with the city but also with a Southern Belle who grew up there. Some time later we were married on Folly Beach, barefoot in the sand. Since that day we have commuted between the rural eastern Netherlands and the southeast of the USA, giving us a feeling of duality about where our home is.

In 2007 the world of improvisational music and writing finally met at the crossroads in my life between Europe and the USA, when I decided to write a book about Scotch single malts and jazz. It was published early 2009 by Charleston's Evening Post Publishing Company, who introduced me to a journalist with a vast knowledge of Jazz: Jack McCray, musician, jazz historian and writer. He agreed to be my contributing editor and the rest is *Whisky & Jazz*.

Not long after the launch in Charleston I felt an almost natural desire to write a story about the Blues and what better than to combine it with another true American icon: bourbon. There it was again, that omnipresent duality: on the one hand the Devil Music and Demon Alcohol. On the other hand the sad music that makes you feel better and the dram a day keeping the doctor away.

The early songsters in the Delta not only sang secular numbers but also religious ones. Among them were preachers, such as the Rev. Gary Davis, famous for his 12-string guitar playing. Some older bluesmen turned to religion in the 1930s and 40s not wanting to play the blues anymore, and then suddenly returned on the scene during the 1960s blues and folk revival. The same goes for distillers, of whom several were lay ministers. Elijah Craig preached the gospel in Kentucky, happily distilling whiskey throughout his life. Dan Call did similar things in Tennessee until his congregation forced him to choose between spirits and the Spirit. He chose the latter and handed his distilling business over to a 14-year-old boy, who would create the most successful whiskey brand in the world. That boy was Jack Daniel, who had learned to distill from Nearest Green, one of Dan Call's slaves. It proves that whiskey is colorblind. It's the same with the blues. B.B. King reportedly said, "I always thought that you had to be double black to play the blues. Then I heard Stevie Ray Vaughan and he was neither."

Duality seems quintessential for the United States: considered the defender of the free world by some, as a global aggressor by others. To me however this wonderful country has become my second home and I thank Americans of all backgrounds for two great gifts: Bourbon and Blues.

Enjoy the read and indulge, preferably in moderation.

Hans Offringa

THE ORIGINS

Straight from the Barrel

When looking at the history of bourbon, one has to first look at the roots of distilling. There are several stories about the origin of distilling and each of them claims to be true. One favorite tale is that of distillation coming from China and travelling via India to the Mideast. Until now no solid evidence is available to fully sustain that theory, other than an artifact found in Mesopotamia, dating back to 3500 BC and thought by archaeologists to be a primitive distilling device. Its purpose might have been the extraction of scents for use in balms and essences.

Then it went all quiet on the Eastern front for thousands of years. In India a fierce liquor called "arrack" was described in writing around 800 BC. A tiny bit closer to home the Greek philosopher Aristotle (384-322 BC) described a natural distillation process when he noticed that salt could be gained from seawater.

St. Patrick (387-461 AD), who made a career from slave to bishop, is often credited with bringing distillation to Ireland, while spreading Christianity at the same time. Another famous spiritual leader, Irish-born St. Columba, could have followed in his footsteps more than a century later, bringing distillation to Scotland when he set foot on Iona in 563. From there Columba traveled between Ireland and the Scottish mainland. If St. Patrick really did know about distilling, how might he have acquired that knowledge?

Egypt could have been the source. Queen Cleopatra

(69-30 BC) knew about distillation and used it among other purposes for manufacturing makeup. The Arabic word *al-kohl* referred to a fine black powder used as a cosmetic. This word now lives on as alcohol. Cleopatra's famous lover and Roman commander Marc Anthony might have been the transmitter to Rome, from where the knowledge was spread over Europe, eventually arriving in Britain. This leads to speculation whether the Scots already knew their dram when St. Columba arrived at Iona. Probably the Irish will immediately protest against this theory, pointing out that Hadrian's Wall (built around 120 AD) prevented such a preposterous idea as distilling coming via England into Scotland. Although Ireland never belonged to the Roman Empire, there is evidence (coins, pottery) of their trading with the Romans as well as scattered Roman raids on the Irish coast. Following that line of reasoning, a passing of distillation techniques from Rome to Ireland is plausible. Interesting theories but they might be qualified as urban legends, lacking clear evidence, especially in the light of accurately documented events that occurred a couple of centuries later in the Middle East.

There were more than 4,000 years between the time that the little clay pot in Mesopotamia was used until written references to distillation techniques showed up in the works of Islamic scholars in North Africa. The most notable authors were Geber, Al-Razi and Avicenna. Geber (721-815 AD), whose full name was Abu Musa Jabir ibn Hayyan was a Renaissance-man *avant la lettre.* Not only was he a well-known physicist, but also a gifted astronomer, alchemist and philosopher. He is widely considered to be the father of Arab chemistry. Geber did groundbreaking work in changing alchemy from magic into real science and is credited for many inventions that form the basis of tools used in chemical laboratories today. One of them is the alembic, of which the copper pot still in many distilleries is a modern form. Some historians claim the alembic was already invented around 200-300 AD, either by Maria the Jewess or Zósimo and Teosebeia of Panoplies, Egyptian alchemists.

Geber was not primarily interested in distilling alcohol. He observed a flammable vapor when distilling, but ultimately tried to create an elixir (from the Arabic *al-iksr*) that could turn one metal into another, preferably lead into gold. Geber described the vapor as "of little use, but of great importance to science." Al-Razi (864-930 AD) however made references to alcohol as a medicine. Avicenna (10th century AD) is reputed to be the first to have used steam distillation. He distilled a mixture of water and rose petals, thus creating the first perfume of modern times: rosewater.

The Moors probably took distilling from North Africa to Spain, where the art was embraced by monasteries and widespread over Western Europe. Several of Geber's writings were translated into Latin, such as the *Kitab al-Kimya* into *The Book of the Composition of Alchemy* (1144) by Robert of Chester. Medieval European scholars used these early writings enthusiastically and concentrated on making alcoholic beverages for medicinal purposes. Michael

Scott (1175-1234) was the first West European scholar and "magician" to define technical distilling terms instead of alchemy in his work *Lumen Luminem*, published in 1225. He taught at the medical school of Salerno, Italy.

Arnoldus Villanova might have picked up distilling on its way to Britain in 1290 when he wrote the first manual on the subject when teaching medicine at the university of Montpellier in France. Around the same time the French Bethunes, a famous family of physicians manifested themselves in Ireland and Scotland as MacBeth or MacBheata (Beaton in England). Legend has it that the MacBheatas originally came to Scotland about 1300 via Ireland with Princess Agnes who married Angus Og Macdonald, Lord of the South Isles, a personal friend of Robert the Bruce – King of Scotland. Patrick Macbeth was doctor to King Robert the Bruce and Rory MacBetha was one of the first physicians to the Lord of the Isles off the southwest coast of Scotland.

The MacBheatas were famous throughout Britain and possessed a huge library of medical books in Gaelic, translated from original Arabic and Greek manuscripts. Since distillation had gradually become the domain of the medical profession, they must have had a thorough knowledge of the process.

The Irish and the Scots more or less agree that the former invented whiskey distilling and the latter the marketing of the drink. Written evidence is available to underwrite that theory. The first recording of distillation in Ireland is a treatise on aqua vitae in *The Red Book of Ossory*, an early 14th century collection of administrative and religious documents compiled by the Bishop of Ossory. The first written record on whisky in Scotland appears almost 200 years later in 1494 and has been quoted many times, "To Friar John Cor, by order of the King, to make aqua vitae, VIII bols of malt." Cor was from Lindores Abbey in the eastern Lowlands. The first complete book on distillation in Europe was written by Hieronymus Braunschweig (Brunswyck), a German scholar, in 1507. Laurence Andrew translated it into English in 1527.

European pioneers, most notably the Irish Scottish, Germans and Dutch brought their distilling techniques with them when they emigrated to the New World about a century after Andrew's translation. The *Speedwell* left Delfshaven in the Netherlands in 1620 and set sail for the shores of southern England to join the *Mayflower*. Together they went on their journey over the Atlantic, but soon the *Speedwell* started leaking seriously. Both ships returned to England, where cargo and pilgrims of the unlucky ship were taken aboard the *Mayflower* and the journey started anew. In December of the same year the pilgrims went ashore at Cape Cod, supposedly because they had ran out of beer. They carried seeds of barley and rye, the former being used for making whisky in Scotland and beer in Germany, the latter for baking bread. However barley proved to be difficult to cultivate in their new surroundings, so they turned their hands to rye. This type of grain was originally considered a weed, since it can grow almost anywhere, even in very poor soil. Thus it became the primary ingredient for the first real American whiskey, known as "Rye" or "Monongahela" – the valley in Pennsylvania where many early pioneers settled. Making whiskey became an extra activity for many farmers, especially during the quiet winter months. The drink became a commodity and was often used for bartering against clothes, food and various other daily needs. Whiskey was easier to transport in a barrel than bushels of grain. It also had a higher street value.

The system of bartering whiskey went on for the following 100 or-so years and the fiery liquid served to boost the morale of the troops in the American Revolutionary War (1776-1791). When the country became independent it was faced with a huge debt and the fresh Federal Government decided it was a good idea to tax whiskey in order to pay off the national debt. For the many small farm distilleries throughout Pennsylvania and Virginia this caused a big problem, since they used whiskey for bartering instead of receiving cash for it. Hence they couldn't pay the imposed tax and chose to ignore it. As a result tax collectors were sent to fine the poor farmers, who then had to travel hundreds of miles to appear in court and pay their debts. They blankly refused. Apart from the fines they didn't want to pay, such a journey was perilous since various hostile territories had to be crossed to reach the capital of Philadelphia. Risking attack by bow and arrows in order to comply with tax regulations didn't go down well with the farm distillers. They revolted, chasing away the tax collectors tarred and feathered, burning down houses of government officials and threatening to kill their families. Of course the Federal Government could not tolerate this Whisky Rebellion, also known as the Whisky Insurrection, and President George Washington sent in his troops to restore law and order. Interestingly enough Washington would later earn a nice extra income distilling and selling whiskey on his plantation in Mount Vernon, Virginia.

Not all farmer distillers revolted and waited for the troops to arrive. A respectable group among them chose to go west, finding new horizons, going further away from the dreaded tax-infused Government. They headed for the western borders of Virginia and ended up in Kentucky, where they not only found fertile grounds but also vast reserves of limestone-filtered clean water, an important asset in making good whiskey. They soon switched to growing corn, the indigenous grain that the Native Americans had given the first pilgrims as a welcome gift in the New Land. Corn contains high levels of starch, which can easily be converted into fermentable sugars. Slowly but surely corn became the dominant grain for making whiskey, although rye, wheat and a small quantity of malted barley were used as supplements. This meant the whiskey could no longer be called "Monongahela" or "rye" for geographical as well as raw material reasons. Instead the whiskey was called bourbon.

The Rev. Elijah Craig (1738-1808) is considered to be the inventor of bourbon and is said to have applied charring the inside of a barrel, enhancing bourbon's sweet taste, for the first time. However there is no evidence of that and there are written references to distillers who

29

had started distilling whiskey earlier than Craig. So, from where does the word bourbon originate? Remarkably, not from the USA, but from Europe. France to be precise. As a thank you for helping the Americans to free themselves from the British yoke in the Revolutionary War, many villages, towns and counties were crowned with French names. Bourbon County, Kentucky refers to the name of the French Royal Family that was in power at the time. Because Bourbon County was much larger in former days, it encompassed many distilleries, including Elijah Craig's, who indeed started using the county name for his whiskey. Today not one commercial distillery lies within the boundaries of the county that gave its name to the most prominent of today's American whiskeys.

During the Civil War (1861-1865) generals on both sides drank whiskey on a daily basis. It was used not only for morale, but also medicinally, often applied as an anesthetic when legs or arms had to be amputated. Abraham Lincoln once said about his general Ulysses Grant, a notorious imbiber of the drink and a strategic genius, "Find out what Grant drinks, I want to send a barrel of it to my other generals."

The American whiskey industry was dealt a severe blow during Prohibition (January 16, 1920 until December 5, 1933). This Noble Experiment, as one government official dubbed it, was instigated half a century earlier by the Christian Women Temperance Movement. In 1874 the WCTU's president, Mrs. Francis Willard, created the first wave of temperance in the USA. Large groups of women took to the streets in organized demonstrations, putting saloons under siege whilst singing psalms and proclaiming texts against the demon alcohol. There certainly was some truth in what they said, illustrated by many a sad example of men spending their entire week's wage on liquor. As a result the women and children suffered hunger, cold and physical abuse. In the person of Francis Willard, the WCTU, an organization that gained a worldwide presence in 1889, had an excellent patron saint. Born in Churchville, NY in 1839, she moved with her family via Ohio to Wisconsin, where she made a solemn pledge at age 10, together with her older sister:

> "To quench our thirst we'll always bring
> Cold water from the well or spring;
> So here we pledge perpetual hate
> To all that can intoxicate."

Willard's protest embraced much more than alcoholic beverages alone, illustrated by the fact that she was one of the initiators of the Polyglot Petition, a huge paper scroll protesting against the abuse of opium and strong liquor. Missionaries collected a stunning two million signatures in fifty different languages on all continents. The scroll was presented to President Cleveland and a copy was sent to the British Queen Victoria. In 1898 Frances Willard passed away and posthumously received a statue in the Statuary Hall of the National Capitol seven years later, being the first women to receive such an honor. It was not rewarded solely because of her interference with alcohol abuse but also for the many humanitarian activities and fundraisers she had organized for the underprivileged and for people suffering religious prosecution.

At its core Willard's approach was a peaceful one. That cannot be said of one of her most fanatic disciples, Cara Amelia Moore. Carry (sometimes spelled Carrie) was born in Kentucky, the heartland of bourbon, in 1846. After an unfortunate marriage with a physician and alcoholic named Charles Gloyd, who managed to drink himself to death a mere month after the wedding, Carry left for Kansas. There she met and married David Nation, a lawyer. Her new surname would become a dreaded word for many a publican. Carry Nation went on a real crusade and not a small one. Now there is nothing wrong with spreading the Gospel as long as it is peaceful and not forced upon people. Carry however had slowly transformed into a religious fundamentalist. She took on the devil himself and was, in her own words, on speaking terms with God, Jesus, the Holy Spirit and a whole bunch of disciples. Her opinion about men was short and harsh, "Men are nicotine-soaked, beer-besmirched, whiskey-greased, red-eyed devils."

On a warm summer day in 1899 Carry Nation directed her first attack ever on the saloon of Mort Strong, in her hometown Medicine Lodge, Kansas. Strong honored his name and threw her out without even flinching. But only a few weeks later, as a direct consequence of her tirades, four of the six saloons in town were closed. Carry Nation rode on the steadily growing wave of the temperance movement - a wave sweeping the USA, Canada and Europe, especially in Scotland, England and Ireland. In February 1900 her quest became more aggressive and she demolished a pharmacy with a sledgehammer, solely because the shop sold brandy. She poured the golden liquid in the gutter and torched it. This event was the starting point for a whole series of destruction in Oklahoma and Kansas. In 1901 Carry used a small hatchet on a raid for the first time, a utensil that would become her trademark. Her radius of action grew and she continued her handiwork as far as California and New York, but changed her modus operandi. She would warn the owner of the targeted saloon with a short letter, reading, "I come to rescue you as well as those that you are murdering. Do not delay, for he that being often reproved hardeneth his neck shall suddenly be destroyed and that without remedy. We invite you to join us in the destruction of the machinery hell has set up here on earth to literally devour humanity."

Those were strong words. Soon her actions were widely reported on the front pages of newspapers in London and New York. After a successful raid Carry Nation was often attacked by people throwing rotten eggs at her, sometimes severely beaten and thrown in jail. That often proved to be a difficult task because Mrs. Nation was six feet three inches and weighed nearly 180 pounds. In her all-black clothes she must have been a threatening sight. One story goes that once it took four policemen to pin her to the ground and arrest her. To pay her fines, Carry's disciples sold souvenirs in the form of a mini-replica of her trademark hatchet, which had become world-famous by now. Various publicans hit back and changed the name of their bars to Carry Nation Saloon. Others developed Carry Nation whiskey bottles in an attempt to humiliate her. These bottles bore a striking resemblance to her figure. It took poor Mr. David Nation 24 years before he had enough of his wife's horrific behavior and filed for divorce on the grounds of abandonment. Meanwhile Carry gathered more disciples who were fueled by her fiery speeches, until she died of a stroke on June 2, 1911.

A considerable number of counties in the USA turned "dry" as the temperance lobby influenced local politicians and subsequently local laws in their favor. Maps from 1910 illustrate the many counties where alcohol was entirely banned. This was not solely the doing of women inspired by religion. At the turn of the 20th century Billy Sunday, a successful baseball player turned Christian, committed himself to the cause for decades to come. He was a real showman and spoke the language of the common folk. One of his much repeated one-liners was "I'm going to knock John Barleycorn out of the box." On stage he took his jacket off and fought an imaginary devil personifying alcohol. The National Prohibition Act was enacted on January 16, 1919 and went into enforcement exactly one year after the bill was passed on January 16, 1920. Then Billy Sunday performed his last act at the "funeral of John Barleycorn." During a service in Norfolk, Virginia, a six-meter long coffin was driven in by horses, followed by a rejected and utterly disappointed devil. The once famous baseball ace welcomed the Nobel Experiment with the words, "Goodbye John. You were God's worst enemy. You were Hell's best friend. I hate you with a perfect hatred."

The boxing world knew a big proponent of alcohol banning too. John L. Sullivan, the Boston Strong Boy, lost the championship match against James J. Corbett in 1892. At first he found solace in heavy drinking but soon repented and converted to Christianity. The teetotalers immediately presented him as "Horrible Example No. 1" – a down-and-out sportsman turned repentant prodigal son.

Public figures and religious zeal were not the only motives that inspired Prohibition. The political powers started to rear their heads too, albeit in back chambers. A person who worked for both camps was the deeply religious William Jennings Bryan, a politician who had been appointed Secretary of State in the Woodrow Wilson government at the start of the 20th century. He'd accepted the job on the one condition that he was not obliged to serve alcoholic drinks during state dinners. Instead he offered the guests water and grape juice.

Originally Bryan advocated free choice for every state regarding Prohibition. Step by step he came to the conviction that the only solution would be a nationwide ban of alcohol. For thirty years he was one of the most popular speakers in the nation addressing the topic of abstinence and he traveled extensively. Unlike Billy Sunday he didn't concentrate on the cities but chose the countryside: the corn belt, the cotton belt and the tobacco belt. In these rural areas his message against Demon Alcohol fell on fertile soil. During a 30-day tour he managed to raise a staggering $400,000 for the Anti Saloon League. He also took care of himself, pocketing $11,000 to pay for his travel expenses.

Bryan was a bit of a loser. When things got tough, his career went downhill. Three times he ran for president and three times he lost. Disaster after disaster followed in an endless stream. He wanted to counterbalance the dollar with silver instead of gold and even enthused a group of Democrats to support this cause, but in the end the proposal was rejected. Bryan voted against a war with Germany and resigned when the USA became involved in World War I. Although Bryan was seen as an eloquent speaker, a great statesman and a powerful leader, in the end he was nicknamed The Champion of Lost Causes. It befitted him since Prohibition, the cause for which he had invested decades of his life, turned out to be a failure from the start. When the Volstead Act was accepted in 1920, Bryan was reduced to a marginal player, standing in the sidelines, watching his country going under in an orgy of booze, corruption and crime.

He didn't live to see Repeal in 1933, dying from a cardiac arrest in 1925 a mere five days after he had acted as District Attorney in a court case fighting Darwinism. During the trial his opponent made it evident that Bryan had not understood the evolution theory at all. The case became internationally famous as The Monkey Trial.

When Bryan changed earthly for eternal life, the horrendous consequences of National Prohibition began to surface. Gangs of murderers and thugs killed each other with unheard of cruel methods and police officers earned a little money on the side looking the other way when illegal drinks were trafficked into cities. The Scots joyfully sustained the illegal smuggling practices by exporting whisky not only to Canada but also to the Bahamas, from where it would find its way illegally into the USA. The most famous smuggler was Captain McCoy, known for his excellent contraband, especially Cutty Sark whisky. His name became a synonym for top quality whiskey. People started asking for The Real McCoy when they wanted uncut whisky.

Private clubs and speakeasies blossomed as never before. Officially the entire country was dry. Government officials regularly found illegal pot stills in the countryside, next to barrels full of whisky. They were destroyed on the spot. Unofficially the USA was wetter than ever. A large speakeasy could easily make a yearly turnover of $500,000 in alcoholic beverages and not one red cent would go into the national treasury. This was another effect of Prohibition. The American nation quickly saw the deficit grow, caused in part by not incurring taxes on alcohol. A rough estimate at the time showed the Federal Government's annual loss at $50,000,000. Financially and morally the Noble Experiment was heading for disaster.

Persons who profited from the situation were gangsters like Al Capone, Bugs Moran, Johnny Torrio, Hymie Weiss and Dion O'Banion. They weren't afraid to attack each other and as a consequence the streets from New York to New Orleans were painted with blood. One of the worst assassinations was executed on Valentine's Day 1929 in

Chicago, when seven members of Bugs Moran's gang were mowed down in an abandoned warehouse by automatic machine guns fired by Capone's cronies. Two of them were dressed like police offers and were responsible for opening the fire. The main target, Bugs himself, escaped since he arrived later at the scene of the crime than planned. Bugs was caught by the authorities soon after and would testify that only Capone could be responsible for such a hideous crime.

The USA had never seen the supposed involvement of police officers in gang wars and was shocked. In Chicago more than 250 police detectives were screened. Since Capone had used hired killers from other parts of the country it was extremely difficult to track them all down. Capone was never convicted for the murders but eventually caught for tax fraud. The most notorious gangster of the USA disappeared behind bars before Prohibition had ended. In 1931 he was sentenced to 11 years in prison. Eight years later he was released early, an ill and broken man. When he eventually died in Florida in 1947 he was poor as a rat. In this particular case crime didn't pay. The man responsible for catching Al Capone was detective Elliot Ness, on whose character a film and a TV-series were built: *The Untouchables.*

The common people weren't really against trafficking of booze by the mafia, but the slaughter on Valentine's Day became a turning point. The public opinion now spoke against the gangsters, who certainly weren't the only ones to blame for the many people that died. Another cause, as dramatic as the gang wars, was the production of so-called bathtub gin, distilled illegally at home. The stuff not only contained methanol, which substance can cause blindness and death, but was regularly diluted with cleaning products and other hazardous liquids. Illegal "distillers" colored the white alcohol with iodine and tobacco to make it look like mature whisky. Thousands of people died after drinking the "rotgut" produced in bathtubs. Even more went blind or suffered permanent paralysis.

The Volstead Act made one exemption on the prohibition of the production, use and sales of alcohol. It was allowed for medicinal purposes only. The ones who were lucky to obtain a license could sell alcohol on a small scale. Medical doctors could write a receipt and the patient acquired his bottle of whisky at the pharmacy. There were many happy patients and doctors during Prohibition. The end came when President Franklin Roosevelt presented a national plan of urgency to the Congress. The 1929 crash in Wall Street and the subsequent depression had decimated the state's finances and that of the citizens, together with a steep decline in morale. The president's New Deal announced a series of measures to help recover the dwindling economy. One of the measures was the Repeal of Prohibition. This happened on December 5, 1933. That same month the Distilled Spirits Institute was founded at Schenley Products Company offices in New York City. This institute still exists and is named Distilled Spirits Council of the United States (DISCUS) since 1973.

The consequences of the 13-year-period of prohibition were also disastrous for the distillers. The damage to the American whiskey industry was enormous. Americans overwhelmingly asked for Scotch. Bourbon was labeled rancid and belonging to the domain of cheap, badly written detective stories. Even in whiskey cocktails, bourbon lost its place to blended whisky. On top of that the film industry in Hollywood used Scotch in most of its movies. Indigenous whiskeys were reduced to the back rooms and bottom shelves. Hardly any bourbon was exported.

Schenley would play an important role in the resurrection of the American alcoholic drinks production, distribution and sales. On the ruins of the Noble Experiment an entire new whiskey industry had to be built. Only a handful of players came to the fore and took care of what still had a chance to survive – a single distillery, a stock of barrels that had escaped the government's urge to destroy, and many famous brand names that were revived by the new distillers elite. This one of the reasons why today Heaven Hill Distillery in Louisville, Kentucky, can present more than 70 different brands on the market.

President Roosevelt also created the Federal Alcohol Control Administration (FACA), which was to write a code of conduct for the distilling industry. Eventually the FACA would dissolve into the Bureau of Alcohol, Tobacco and Firearms. At first each state could define its own rules regarding production and sales of alcoholic beverages, which lead to a myriad of laws, frequently contradicting one another. For instance one state would specify that liquor could only be sold to customers with food, whilst another state would forbid that combination. When Frank Kane published his *Anatomy of the Whisky Business* in 1965, to show what had been accomplished in the thirty years after Repeal, many of the state laws were still in use. Over time things have been standardized, more or less, but the construction with Federal and State Law still makes it virtually impossible to impose one national law. Today in various states the sale of alcohol is a state monopoly and in other states liquor stores are private enterprises. To organize whisky tastings in Seattle, Washington, one has to deal with a civil servant to get a permit, where in Charleston, South Carolina, a restaurant owner can organize it himself, as long as he posses a license to serve strong alcohol. For distillers it is a nightmare to register a new product   nationwide. Due to the various laws in the different states he needs at least 27 different labels.

Today some states and counties in the USA are still "dry," among which parts of Tennessee. Moore County, home to Jack Daniel Distillery, is one of them. The neighboring county is allowed to sell however, so people hop over to Lincoln County, buy their stash and return to Lynchburg. The millions of visitors to Jack Daniel have to be content with a lemonade or water at the end of their tour – no tasting the product on site.

Remarkably enough the rise of the Scottish single malt whiskies at the end of the 1980s also signaled a turning point for the American whiskey industry. The consumer became interested in bourbon again and discovered along the way that American distillers produced beautiful, mature whiskeys. Fine bourbons slowly but steadily resurfaced. The renewed interest in American whiskey led to the production of "small batch whiskeys." American distillers today experiment with new varieties and bottle limited quantities of rye whiskey, wheated whiskey and even single malts. In the last decade rye whiskey has had a revival, but its output is minimal next to bourbon and Tennessee whiskey.

George Washington's original distillery in Mount Vernon has been reconstructed and made part of the American Whiskey Trail, a major tourist attraction and serious pilgrimage route for many aspiring whiskey drinkers. The equipment in use at Mount Vernon strongly resembles the tools invented by the Arabic scientist Geber. So in a way, one could argue that the roots of American distilling are to be found in North Africa. Coincidentally the roots of the blues are to be found on the same continent...

How Blue Can You Get?

Various writers and scholars agree that the roots of the blues can be found in Western Africa, but they disagree in what way today's blues is similar to the traditional forms of music still performed throughout Africa.

There is clear evidence that blues' roots are to be found in African folk music, brought to America from the west coast of Africa. During the crossing, slaves were forced to sing and dance on the decks by the captain or boatswain. Often in African music, singing and dancing are united, but this was a cruel use of an age-old custom. The exercise was supposed to keep them fit because they would be sold upon their arrival. It was also meant to boost their morale since the circumstances on board were horrific and a large percentage of the human cargo did not arrive in the New World. The slaves held no possessions, not even their basic instruments – a wooden drum, a one-string guitar and the halam, a five-string instrument today recognized as being the father of the American banjo. They could only use the instrument they were born with – their voice.

African folk music existed in various forms of expression: religious chants that accompanied rituals, secular songs sung to make monotonous labor easier, and storytelling by wandering musicians, called "griots" or "bards". These were the musical formats brought to America and they would serve as the basis upon which the blues were to develop into the father of all modern popular music.

After being sold, many enslaved Africans were taken to the plantations of the Deep South and made to work. The foreman would encourage them to sing when performing manual labor, such as plowing the fields or picking cotton. Since the slaves must have dearly missed their home, freedom and family left behind, the songs were usually sorrowful and contained themes of homesickness, desolation, a broken heart or maltreatment. They carried an implicit message to get away, to travel as far as possible from the people that harmed them, to escape from the everyday misery. On the other hand, there was no place to go, so the music itself became a form of escape. In their scarce free time the slaves continued to make music, using whatever utensil they could lay their hands on to transform it into an instrument. Pots, pans and wooden sticks served as percussion. A string tied to a doorpost between two nails with a bottleneck under the string for tuning purposes created a copy of the guitar they had left in Africa. When working in the fields, slaves would perform in unison, in a call and response format, often singing with the rhythm of the work being performed, thus easing the flow of work and synchronizing their motions. When at leisure, the individual musician's craft had a chance: songs evolved and became more elaborate. A soloist-chorus dynamic was created. However, the subject matter stayed the same and the music remained a route of escape from the burdens of an oppressive daily life.

After the abolishment of slavery in the 1860s, African Americans gradually obtained more freedom and gained possessions, including musical instruments. Many also gained an increased freedom of movement, even changing venues completely, thus widening their environment and altering their relationship to it. At the same time that this was a positive change, it rendered their day-to-day lives more exposed to external forces. There were more and different opportunities to "get the blues."

They first turned to the guitar, an easy instrument to carry. This music was recorded for posterity: in 1867 *Slave Songs of the United States* was published. Unfortunately the end of slavery didn't end the misery of the African Americans living on plantations. They still had little choice and many entered into indentured servantships bearing an unfortunate resemblance to their former state. By federal law they were free, but racist legislation was passed by individual states, predominantly in the South. There African Americans were restricted in travel, forbidden to eat with white persons or to vote. It fueled their anger but at the same time their creativity with song texts displaying more variety. The six-string guitar became the favorite instrument for accompanying solo singing, the harmonica often added rhythm. Both were highly portable and suitable for intense traveling. The old work song slowly evolved into what we now recognize as Delta Blues.

Why Delta blues? In 1903 composer and trumpet player W.C. Handy supposedly heard an African American guitarist playing a song, using his knife on the neck of the guitar to create a special sound effect, later to become known as bottleneck or slide guitar. This moment in time is generally considered as the discovery of the blues. The encounter took place at a little railway station in a fertile delta, where the Yazoo and Mississippi rivers join. It inspired Handy to compose a tune and have it published as sheet music in 1911. The name of this piece is "The Memphis Blues" and it is considered by many the first ever published bluesy music. In 1914 Handy published another tune that would become world-famous as "St. Louis Blues." Both tunes were performed by jazz orchestra and not by individual musicians. At the time African American musicians were not allowed to record music. Hence sheet music performed by orchestras was the way to have this music heard by large audiences.

Handy advertised himself as the Father of the Blues, but that seems rather overstated. Although he popularized the blues by playing tunes in a jazzy setting with a big band, it was a far cry from the music that single guitar player had made at the railway station in northwest Mississippi. At the time, and most likely much earlier, there must have been dozens, or maybe even hundreds of similar musicians playing and singing in that specific area. This particular part of Mississippi contained a large and very poor African American population that drew on its innate talents to find some form of free entertainment. In neighboring states Texas and Louisiana similar musical developments were under way, but not in concentrations as high as in the Delta, simply because the populations were much smaller and so was the musical reservoir to draw from. In the more jazz-influenced cities New Orleans and Charleston, South Carolina a blues form developed called Piedmont blues. It was infused with ragtime music and here the piano started to play a role in the development of the blues.

Things changed rapidly when singer Mamie Smith recorded the song "Crazy Blues" in 1920. It meant the start of a whole series of recordings for African American artists. Interestingly the first to profit from this were mostly female singers, such as Ma Rainey, Bessie Smith, Sippie Wallace, Ida Cox, Bertha "Chippie" Hill and Victoria Spivey. From the Delta rose a steady stream of talented guitarists and singers, helped by early music scouts like H.C. Speir, who set up a recording studio in Jackson, Mississippi. The scouts scoured the countryside trying to find real talent - and succeeded. In Texas, Blind Lemon Jefferson emerged; in Louisiana the jazzier oriented Lonnie Johnson. However, it was in the Delta that the most talented of them all was found: Charlie Patton, by many considered the real father of the Delta blues. With the success of his first records, the fans craved for more and the talent scouts were more than happy to find new stars.

In the second half of the 1920s up to the mid 1930s many famous Delta blues men were discovered and recorded, among whom Son House, Ishmon Bracey, Skip James, Lightnin' Hopkins, Bukka White and Robert Johnson. They all traveled to perform their music, usually for small audiences in juke joints, accompanying themselves. Patton was known not only for his mastering of the guitar and powerful songs but for showmanship too, playing his guitar behind his back or plucking the strings with his mouth. He also liked to drink whiskey and chase women, often married ones, and get into fights over them: recurring topics in many blues songs. Patton was known to be extremely straightforward and rude to the point of insulting people. No wonder he was often involved in disputes like many of his fellow bluesmen. If they committed serious crimes they were put away in the Delta's Parchman prison farm. Many songs were born in that prison or refer to it, like Bukka White's "Parchman Blues." Scouts would even go so far as to ask the prison warden permission to access the grounds in their never-ending quest for natural born blues talents. "Jail House Blues" made famous by Elvis Presley in the 1950s probably had its origins at Parchman Farm.

Some Delta blues talents were overseen at first, only to be recognized later. This was two-fold, partly due to the migration of African Americans out of the Delta, and partly due to the end of Prohibition. Many African Americans moved to northern and midwestern cities searching for work during the 1920s and 1930s. The migration had a number of reasons, including the mechanization of cotton picking, which caused massive unemployment, carrying out the same amount of work as 30 laborers per day. The repressive post-Reconstruction Jim Crow laws and customs were motivators also. The Great Depression added to the flight away from rural and agricultural areas, with more work opportunities in urban areas. During Prohibition, many bars closed, and those that remained open often had no live music, not wishing to attract attention. When Prohibition ended in 1933, live music in bars became popular again and recording of new artists diminished, further to be damaged in popularity by radio broadcasting.

With the Great Trek to the cities the blues gradually changed. In the 1940s music could be amplified and the invention of the electric guitar caused the volume to increase. The role of the guitar changed from rhythmic accompaniment to creator of melody. Percussion was added by means of trap drums and electric bass, slowly favored over the acoustic standing bass. Piano and keyboards were added whilst the saxophone regularly replaced or supplemented the blues harp, sometimes known as a "Mississippi sax."

Chicago Blues was born. The old Delta blues musicians didn't perform anymore, sometimes due to conversion to Christianity or perhaps not wanting to be reminded of their slave ancestry. The ones who did try to play in the cities were often dismissed as being old-fashioned and they returned disillusioned to the Delta, practicing their musicianship on the farm, playing in solitude on the porch after a working day.

The electric blues meant the rise to stardom for those overlooked Delta musicians: B.B. King, Muddy Waters, Howlin' Wolf and John Lee Hooker. They would all show up in Chicago, albeit that King and Hooker had made a detour first, respectively via West Memphis and Detroit. More young white people became interested in this powerful, structured music and the Delta blues went into a steep decline. A few diehards like Alan Lomax and Gayle Dean

Wardlow, scouting and recording in the Deep South, documented the living remains of the Delta blues.

With the coming of Jerry Lee Lewis and Elvis Presley some blues drifted in a different direction, which led Muddy Waters to write the famous song "The Blues Had a Baby and They Named It Rock and Roll." This musical style was pioneered by Chuck Berry who became a great inspiration to the Rolling Stones in the early 1960s. Interestingly enough, at the turn of the 1950s the Delta blues was rediscovered and became popular again with a wide audience, initially caused by the aforementioned scouts in the Delta, in search of blues' roots. They found that some of the old guys were still alive and persuaded Mississippi John Hurt, Bukka White, Skip James and Son House to come and perform at Folk/Blues Festivals in Newport and Ann Arbor, playing alongside a young Bob Dylan and other folkies.

On the other side of the Atlantic, young aspiring guitar players the likes of Eric Clapton, Jimmy Page and Keith Richards picked up the songs of Robert Johnson and turned them into their own electric renditions. Son House and Bukka White, as well as Muddy Waters, B.B. King, Howlin' Wolf and harmonica wizard Sonny Boy Williamson II crossed the ocean to play their blues with English musicians or brought their bands with them, to the amazement of an entirely new audience.

In Los Angeles at the end of the 1960s the first white rock blues band was born: Canned Heat, performing with Son House and recording an album with John Lee Hooker, called *Hooker 'n' Heat*. The name of the band was derived from illegally distilled liquor during Prohibition.

Texas spawned unforgettable guitarists such as Johnny Copeland, Albert Collins, Jimmy and Stevie Ray Vaughan. In the UK Jimmy Page, who had recorded for years with many blues men as a studio musician, formed Led Zeppelin and launched hard rock from a blues platform in 1968, their first two albums drawing heavily on old blues songs like "I Can't Quit You Baby" and "Killing Floor." Zeppelin would become an inspiration to many modern day blues and rock groups, although the group conveniently forgot to credit the original authors of various songs.

John Lennon once remarked in an interview that he wished he could play like BB King. Various Beatles songs are firmly grounded in the blues, as are all popular music styles. Whether disguised as country music, bluegrass, rock 'n' roll, soul, funk, gospel, pop, disco, punk, reggae, rock, heavy metal, hip hop, rap or jazz, the blues is their common denominator, their true musical father. Jazz and blues still hold much in common, albeit that the latter, even today, is the more closely connected to the original African roots.

The reason the blues evolved in America might not only be because enslaved Africans were there in large numbers and brought with them the attributes of music that would provide a vehicle for expressing their pain. The blues is an expression of the trials and tribulations and joys and celebrations of the individual within the context of the group. Individualism is probably best illustrated in North America, in the context of world's history. Everybody suffers, to one degree or another, every day, everywhere in the world, small and large victories and losses. That's why the blues resonates everywhere. But the potential for suffering seems directly proportionate to the extent of individual freedom a person has. There is more chance to fail, the more freedom you have to try something – woo a lover, make money, fulfill one's self, cross the street, get love and attention, please others, pay the bills, etc.

The blues is definitely not merely a pity-seeking reaction to oppression. It is proactive. It is well within (African) social traditions. Taking on the blues is a deliberate behavioral action. You invite the blues to chase the blues. The amalgamation of the culture of Africans with the culture of their oppressors created a new art form, arming the oppressed with a means to sustain themselves and have a chance at improving their circumstances. The fact that the blues today is a globally accepted form of musical expression confirms that this fusion also applies to different socio-cultural circumstances in other parts of the world. With regard to the once enslaved Africans, the real sorrow songs were the spirituals, the root of African American music, the first form to combine elements from Africa and America. The blues was the next major step on the evolutionary scale of African American music, further crystallizing the hope that can come out of sorrow. It's not only pain medicine; it's an elixir for joy.

***

Bourbon and blues both originated in an agricultural environment as a byproduct of corn and cotton. They both resisted authority. They both went into steep declines but managed to resurface time and again. Prohibition nor Depression nor Segregation could kill them. They left their birth grounds to settle elsewhere. Today not a commercial whiskey distillery is found in Bourbon County and the blues music industry is far removed from the Delta. However both icons toured the world and took center stage, not to be thrown off. I think they do well together.

Time to do a sound-check.

THE INSTRUMENTS

From the Grain to the Bottleneck

Bourbon, like music, is composed. Not with scores, but with something called the mash bill. It is a recipe the trade uses that specifies the exact ingredients needed. Bourbon is made from a mixture of grains, such as corn, wheat, rye and barley.

When barley is malted, natural enzymes are formed, which help to convert the starch into fermentable sugars. Generally speaking we distinguish two types of barley: two-row, with one row of seeds on each side of the halm; and six-row, with three rows of seeds on each side. The former type is mainly grown in Scotland and Ireland. The USA grows both types. Each type is subdivided into many different varieties. Cultivating new barley varieties is a continuous process. Barley is prone to picking up fungi, even barley that was originally resistant. If a new variety performs well, the whiskey industry might exchange it for its previous barley. Some distillers are convinced that the type of barley influences the taste of the eventual whiskey. However, the general assumption in the trade is that the type of barley is barely a factor of importance in regards to taste. Usually the price is the deciding factor, although the malting plants do have to deliver the malt to their customers' exact specifications. Order descriptions are detailed to the point of expected yield of alcohol per ton barley taken in. Barley gives a creamy character and depth to whiskey, often identifiable as the taste of sweet biscuits and malt.

Rye originated in Europe and was long considered a weed. Slowly it was put to use for distilling strong liquors, mainly in Germany, Poland, Russia and Scandinavia. Pioneers who left for the Americas in the 18th century took rye and their distilling knowledge with them. The majority settled in Pennsylvania. They were called "Pennsylvania Dutch," a name still in use. However, those pioneers weren't Dutch, but German. The English-speaking Americans confused "Deutsch" with "Dutch." A practical characteristic of rye is the fact that it can grow almost anywhere, even in poor and exhausted soil. In the beginning American whiskey was rye whiskey, everywhere in the USA. Rye renders a spicy and fruity taste to whiskey, with a clearly recognizable scent of peppermint.

Native Americans used to grow an entirely different, indigenous crop that could be found all over the vast new world and was not known in Europe at the time: corn (or maize). The Indians presented this crop to the pioneers as a welcome gift and they knew what to do with it.

Today the vast majority of American whiskey, whether it be bourbon or Tennessee, is distilled from a mash of corn, rye and/or wheat, with the addition of a small amount of malted barley, which acts as a catalyst with the forming of enzymes. The ratio is written down on the mash bill. With bourbon it is mainly corn (at least 51%). The higher the percentage of corn, the sweeter and fatter, but also sharper the eventual whiskey. Above 80% corn on the mash bill, the distillate is called corn whiskey.

Wheat has been grown in Europe for centuries but was

only introduced to the USA in the 19th century. The most important states that grow and harvest wheat are Indiana, Kansas, Kentucky, Nebraska and Ohio. Wheat in itself does not generate a whiskey's sweetness, but rather promotes it. Much of the sweet flavor found in bourbon comes from the natural sugars present in the white oak barrels, and wheat being less flavorful than rye, allows more of these natural sweeteners to show through in the bottled product. Maker's Mark is a beautiful example and this whisky (written without the "e") is also called wheated bourbon. In Scotland for many years corn was used to distill grain whisky, the main component in blended Scotch. Over the last decades corn has almost entirely been replaced by wheat, due to financial reasons.

There are some rules that must be adhered to when producing straight bourbon. Since this is not a book about distilling, I won't delve into the intricacies of that venerable art but will instead summarize the essentials.

The mash bill of straight bourbon must contain at least 51% corn but no more than 80%, with the addition of wheat or rye and a small portion of malted barley. The mixture is milled and then put in an industrial atmospheric cooker. Hot water is added. The malted barley acts as a catalyst to form enzymes. These enzymes promote the conversion of starch into fermentable sugars. The sugars dissolve in the mash and a sugary liquid, resembling a thick kind of porridge is the result. It is then transferred to a vessel called wash back or fermentation tank. Yeast is added which converts the sugars into alcohol and carbon dioxide. The eventual liquid contains approximately 8-10% alcohol by volume (ABV) and can be compared with a strong beer. In fact, the first phase of whiskey distilling is akin to brewing beer, without the addition of hops.

The next step is the distilling of the alcoholic fluid. This usually happens in two rounds (excepting, for example, Woodford Reserve and various micro-distillers). The first round takes place in a column still, called the beer still in the industry. They vary dramatically in diameter, height and material from distillery to distillery, typically soaring several stories high. The bottom section of the beer still, below the feed plate, separates the alcohols and congeners from the grains. At the top of the beer still is the rectification section in which the 8%-10% ABV fluid is generally increased to between 62.5% and 75% ABV. The beer stills are usually made of copper; other material would allow sulfur to pass through to the final product. When sulfur (from the water source) comes in contact with copper in the beer still, copper-sulfate is collected on the interior walls of the still in the form of a black residue. Distillers shut their distilling operations down once or twice a week to clean this residue from the still. The second round happens in a copper pot still, generally called a doubler because it is where the second distillation takes place, not because ABV doubles here. In the case of Jim Beam it is a "thumper," which is the same as a doubler except the vapor from the beer still is not super-cooled prior to entering the doubler and when the vapor comes in contact with the liquid in the vessel it causes the copper walls to expand with a thumping sound. The stills are usually heated by steam. Alcohol has a lower boiling point than water, so the alcohol fumes rise to the neck of the still and are captured in a condenser – a kind of cooler – and return to a liquid state.

The resulting liquid should contain no more than 80% ABV and will usually be diluted to 62.5% ABV before being stored for maturation, although some distillers use different percentages. The colorless liquid is pumped into new wooden barrels made of the American white oak, charred from the inside. The barrels are charred to open up the hard, dense oak, giving two important aspects to the whiskey. First, this provides the natural color for the whiskey found in a bottle. Second, it opens the pores of the wood, allowing the liquid to penetrate the wood during the maturation process, picking up the natural sugars present in the wood. Maturation takes a minimum of two years but most bourbons mature at least four years. The temperature in the warehouses changes remarkably between summer and winter, especially in Kentucky and Tennessee. When hot, the liquid expands into the barrel, when cold it retracts. Oak barrels are porous and breathe; part of the liquid evaporates and ascends to heaven - that's why it is called the Angels' Share.

Before being bottled the whiskey is diluted again, by law to not less than 40% ABV. In the USA, proof is another way to describe ABV. Rule of thumb: divide proof by two to calculate the alcohol percentage by volume. Some distillers bottle bourbon at higher percentages, such as the Wild Turkey 101 (50.5% ABV) or even at cask strength.

When the bottle is empty, keep the neck. It might come in handy when you want to play some blues. . . .

From the Songster to the Big Band

As bourbon is defined in the mash bill, blues is defined by rules too. The first American blues musicians are called songsters. The emphasis was on their voices and they would accompany themselves with simple household tools like pots and pans, jugs, wash boards and a diddley bow – a derivative of the ancient African one-string guitar – usually made of a plank, two nails and a string, and a bottleneck for tuning the string. When they could afford it, they would buy a secondhand six-string guitar or a harmonica.

The early songs had a simple form. The first sentence would be repeated almost exactly and the third one would be different but rhyming with the previous one, thus forming an A-A-B format, for example:

Last night I was drinking, I was drinkin' shine
Oh yeah, last night, last night I was drinkin' shine
But today I wish this sore old head it wasn't mine

The melody was based on a pentatonic or five-tone scale, common in Africa, but different from the diatonic or eight-tone scale used in most of the Western world. The duration of the song and the meter were shortened or lengthened whenever the performer felt like it. A typical African musical tradition is the "bending "of notes – the effect that creates the distinct "blue note" which defines the blues (and its offspring jazz). The early 20th century traveling blues musician usually played alone and didn't have to conform his style to accompanying players.

Topics were invariably homesickness, travel, departure, broken hearts, infidelity, a hard life, but with an undertone of humor and a double meaning. The double meaning might have originated from the old work songs and spirituals, when the slaves wanted to communicate something in the fields, which was not meant to be understood by their overseers. Sometimes they had a sexual innuendo and some could be rather explicit. The songs were sad but meant to make you feel better, to lift you up from your misery. A whisky metaphor is consuming some of "the hair of the dog that bit you," i.e. taking a drink to stave off the bad effects of previous drinking.

In the early 1900s the Delta or country blues started to evolve in different directions. Call and response forms would drift into the direction of religious songs and gospels, still heard in today's churches. Musicians began playing together; so-called jug bands were formed, small groups using the same household items as their ancestors on the plantations did. The Piedmont blues from Richmond, VA through Charleston, SC and Atlanta, GA transformed into ragtime, with the piano as the instrument of choice.

Ensembles emerged out of the early jug bands, the added horns giving a certain swing and jazzy feeling to the blues as can be heard in Louis Jordan's Jump Blues introduced in the late 1930s. Count Basie and his big band The Barons of Rhythm emerged in Kansas City and played jazz that was heavily marinated in the blues. This popular-ized the saxophone as a replacement for the harmonica in many blues bands. These developments would later in-spire B.B. King to form his own band with saxes, trumpets and trombones.

The original instruments of the early blues, song and guitar, were still in place. Bessie Smith recorded her songs without drums or other percussion instruments. With her excellent feel for rhythm and strong voice she didn't need any. When the early Delta blues musicians migrated to the cities they encountered amplification of sound and the electric guitar. They started to perform with other musi-cians in clubs. Since they weren't constantly on the road anymore, they could enhance their performances with in-struments that were more stationary than guitar and har-monica, such as piano and the drum kit.

The development from solo performance to group per-formance also created the need for a more structured ap-proach and duly the 12-bar blues in 4/4 became the norm, although slow blues is often performed in 3/4.

Today a blues band might have various acoustic and electric guitars, keyboards, drums, harmonica, horns. Rare but not unheard of are violin, mandolin and banjo, although the latter three are more common in bluegrass, one of those close relatives of the blues. But from where do these instruments originally come?

Our voice is a gift from God and need not be analyzed any further. We all have one, all are suitable for singing, but not all are suitable to be heard...

Then the guitar. Originally slaves played the diddley bow, their version of an ancient African one-string instrument. Only after slavery, they started using the six-string and sometimes even 12-string guitar as we know it today. This six-string acoustic guitar that would become the main companion of the early blues travelers comes from Europe. Its origins are rather fuzzy. Guitars might have been around since the 15th century, used as a replacement for the lute, which was more complicated to play. These acoustic guitars grew up in the realm of classical music. Various scholars state that it originated from Spain. This early guitar entered the New World in the 16th century. In the 1800s it was modified and enhanced, gaining a much larger body than the earlier versions.

The electric guitar, however, is an American invention. The first effort to build one was executed by Mr. Lloyd Lear, around 1923. His invention, an electrostatic pick-up was not a success. In 1931 Adolph Rickenbacker and George Beauchamp mounted an electromagnetic pick-up upon a lap-steel guitar and created the first commercially available model. It became known as the frying pan. At the turn of the 1930s this technology was adapted to the classic Spanish guitar. In the 1940s the instrument was developed further by the likes of Les Paul and Leo Fender. The double bass went along with the development of electric guitars and would be replaced by the electric bass guitar starting in the mid 1940s, although some bass players, most notably Willie Dixon, continued to play the upright acoustic bass well into the 1980s.

The harmonica is far older and has its roots in a Chinese instrument from as early as the 14th century BC. Called a sheng, it is made with bamboo reeds and plays an important role in traditional Asian music. It was first imported to Europe at the turn of the 18th century and soon various European instrument makers started using different materials to build them. The most successful among them was Matthias Hohner who learned to build harmonicas from two German clockmakers. He is also responsible for exporting the small but versatile instrument to the USA, as early as 1862. His original diatonic harmonica had 10 holes and by drawing air in and blowing it out, one could produce 20 different notes. Later Hohner invented the chromatic harmonica with a button on the side, making it possible to play all notes. In the USA the first bluesmen who became well known as expert harmonica players surfaced primarily in the 1930s. Among them John Lee, aka "Sonny Boy" Williamson, Rice Miller, aka "Sonny Boy Williamson II," Big Walter Horton and Little Walter. Today there are still great blues harmonica players, for example James Cotton, Kim Wilson and Sugar Blue, the latter appropriately nicknamed the "Charlie Parker of the Blues Harp." And not to forget the world famous Belgian harmonica wizard Toots Thielemans who once said in an interview with jazz/blues historian Jack McCray, "The blue note is a gift from African Americans that I am truly thankful for. It is like a tear that can make you cry or make you laugh."

The piano as we know it today is derived from age-old percussion instruments on which hammers were used to strike strings - hammered dulcimers. The first European attempts to build stringed keyboard instruments were undertaken in the Middle Ages. By the 17th century two main types became common in the performance of classical music: the clavichord and the harpsichord, respectively struck by tangents and plucked by quills. The Italian instrument maker Bartolomeo Cristofori is credited with being the father of the modern pianoforte. Three of his pianos, dated about 1720, survive today. The Massachusetts Gazette of March 21, 1771 mentions a piano in America for the first time, in an announcement of a concert, "select pieces on the forte piano and guitar."

Over time various modifications improved the instrument. Erard invented a small mechanical device making it possible to strike a hammer successively rather than waiting for it to return to its starting position before being struck again. With that invention, the musician could play faster if he chose. Babcock devised a cast iron frame from one piece, replacing the previously used wooden frame, patenting his invention in 1825 in Boston, MA. Because it was far more solid, thicker strings could be attached to it. This not only influenced the dynamics and the sound, but the piano was more robust. One of the consequences of these improvements is the fact that many people have a piano at home today. The standard piano has 88 keys, 36 black and 52 white with a reach of seven octaves and a minor third. The electric piano stems from the 1920s, but became popular in the late 1960s and early 1970s with blues-rock, funk and jazz musicians, and also in the realm of pop music. Billy Preston can be heard playing a Fender Rhodes piano on the Beatles' song "Get Back." Eventually the electric piano evolved into the synthesizer and later the digital piano.

The piano is considered a percussion instrument and this leads us to the origins of the drum. For fear of digressing, I will condense the origins of the drum itself by stating that drums might have been preceded by hand clapping as a means of communication and accompaniment, skip the development of the single drum in various places around the world and focus on the development of the drum kit in the USA.

The first loosely assembled drum assortments occurred in late 19th century American brass bands that usually had two or three drummers playing a snare drum, cymbals and a bass drum. When the snare drum stand and base drum pedal were invented in the early 1900s, a single drummer could play polyrhythmic. It was American percussionist William Ludwig Sr. who founded the Ludwig Drum Company in Chicago in 1909 and the first drum kit was a fact. With the 1920s came the hi-hat, originally known as a low-boy, consisting of two opposing cymbals and a foot pedal. In New Orleans drummers began using fly swatters that would evolve into brushes. With the coming of swing bands in the 1930s rose the need for a larger drum kit. Percussionist Gene Krupa is credited with expanding the base kit into an assortment that is still popular with many drummers, since it is relatively easy to set up and move around: a 24" or 26" bass drum, a 14" snare drum, a small tom mounted on the shell of the bass drum, a 16" floor tom, three cymbals in various sizes and a hi-hat. Krupa was also instrumental in the development of tunable tom toms in conjunction with the Slingerland Drum Company, whose drums he used his entire career. In the mid 1950s Remo Beli invented the plastic drum head and the calfskin drum head gradually disappeared in favor of Beli's invention, which required less tuning than the organic cover that tended to shrink in dry weather. Wooden drumstick tips were replaced with nylon tips. In the 1960s the cymbals became more important and grew bigger. The 1970s witnessed the appearance of open or concert toms (without a bottom) and Ludwig introduced acrylic drum shells. Legendary Led Zeppelin drummer John Bonham was among the first to use them. In the 1970s the memory lock was introduced as a system to adjust the height of the stands by means of a stopping device, followed by a 1980s invention called Resonance Isolation Mounting System, which improved resonance. The number of drums and tom toms grew and electronic devices were added. Today complete electronic drum kits are available, stretching the limits and the imagination, but far removed from the standard drum kit used in the blues.

Of all the horns and wind instruments, the saxophone is the most used in the blues; in many cases it replaced the harmonica and the kazoo. The saxophone was invented by Adolphe Sax, the son of a 19th century Belgian instrument maker. In 1841 the sax made its debut at an exhibition in Brussels. It is a relatively new instrument compared with the other ones mentioned in this chapter. Adolphe managed to invent a stunning 14 variations on the instrument of which eight survive today, but only four are common: the soprano, alto, tenor and baritone saxophone. Originally the saxophone was used in classical music. Coleman Hawkins is credited with introducing the saxophone to the world of blues and jazz with his seminal recording "Body and Soul." Another veteran of the bluesy sax is Eddy Cleanhead Vinson. While made of brass, the sax is in fact a single reed woodwind instrument and is a close cousin to the clarinet. Most blues is played on the alto and tenor saxophones.

Enough of history, now let's do some serious jammin' and drammin"!

THE PLAYLIST

Preacher Blues
Elijah Craig and Skip James

Many bourbons have been named after legendary pioneers of American distilling history. Sometimes distillery and brand bear the same name. Usually however that is not the case. Famous brands that were around before Prohibition ended up in the hands of businessmen who built new distilleries after Repeal. Those distilleries frequently changed their name, to make it even more complicated for writer and reader. Well, interesting too, if tracing the history of a particular distillery is something you do for a living!

One man who made his life's work from that kind of research was Sam K. Cecil (1918-2005). After his retirement in 1980 he dedicated 20 years of his life to a book with the clear and descriptive title *The Evolution of The Bourbon Whiskey Industry in Kentucky*. This publication is an inspiration to many whisky writers and an almost inexhaustible source for tracking down interesting facts. Like the following story about Elijah Craig, the 18th century reverend and Renaissance man who was eventually immortalized as a whiskey brand by Heaven Hill Distilleries.

Elijah Craig was born in Orange County, Virginia, in 1743 and started his working life as a tobacco farmer. After some time his "need for a Christian Religion" was awakened by two Baptist preachers, David Thomas and Samuel Harris. They organized meetings in Craig's tobacco barn and Craig was ordained a reverend in 1771. Elijah and two of his brothers preached the Gospel in an interpretation that was a bit too loose for Virginian members of the Church of England. So the brothers moved to the neighboring area of Kentucky in 1785 to escape prosecution for their "heretic" ideas. An interesting fact: the pilgrim fathers exchanged Europe for America for similar reasons.

Elijah Craig's plan was to build a kind of Christian Utopia in Big Spring, Scott County and call it Lebanon. He turned out to be a real builder, revealing many talents. Next to his religious tasks he managed to build roads and bridges, speculated with land, owned and operated a corn mill, produced hemp rope, made paper and...distilled whiskey, which he had done previously in Virginia. Elijah Craig is often credited with the honorary title "Father of Bourbon," since he is supposed to have been the first distiller to char his barrels before filling them with whiskey and transporting them via the Mississippi River to New Orleans. During that journey the whiskey developed a desirable taste and color. Nowadays among other laws regulating what may or may not be called straight bourbon is the one requiring that the newly distilled spirit aka "white dog" mature in new, charred, oak barrels.

Craig died in 1808. An obituary in the Kentucky Gazette stated clearly that a remarkable man had left the building, "If virtue consists in being useful to our fellow citizens, perhaps there were few more virtuous men than Mr. Craig."

Old Heaven Hill Springs Distillery is the original name of Heaven Hill, a distillery that can trace back its history to

1935. One of the founders was Joe Beam, a member of the famous whiskey dynasty that goes by the same name, and cousin of James "Jim" Beauregard Beam, who was responsible for building that brand name. Joe's fellow founders were Dick Nolan, Harlan Mathis, Marion Muir and the Shapira brothers Gary, George, Ed, Dave and Mose. After World War II the five brothers bought the shares of the other founders to get Heaven Hill in one family, albeit that they kept a Beam as master distiller.

Over the next couple of decades Heaven Hill steadily expanded, acquiring warehouses and brands from other distilleries, increasing its market share considerably. On the outskirts of Bardstown, KY, it became busy with trucks loading and un-loading barrels of whiskey at the distinctive high rising, grey-colored warehouses. The whiskey produced was sold on the market under various names, with a remarkable preference for names of whiskey pioneers from the 18th and 19th century: J.W. Dant, Ezra Brooks, Henry McKenna and J.T.S. Brown, just a few of the more than 90 brands that are currently made and marketed by Heaven Hill, which in turn lends its name from 18th century distiller William Heavenhill.

1986 witnessed the launch of a 12-year-old small batch bourbon under the brand name Elijah Craig. It was a vatted bourbon, made from 100 especially selected barrels. A remarkably delicate bourbon, especially considering its age. It is a genuine beauty, with vanilla, fruit, a suggestion of peppermint and oak notes in the background and a medium long finish. In 1992 the 12-year-old received company from an 18-year-old expression, currently one of the oldest single barrel bourbons on the planet and even more beautiful than its sibling.

Not everything went well with Heaven Hill. On November 7, 1996 one of the warehouses caught fire. The consequences were devastating. The hungry flames consumed seven warehouses and the distillery itself was damaged beyond repair. The source of the fire remains a mystery, since all possible evidence simply melted. In the end 105,000 barrels of whiskey were lost, almost 15% of the total amount of whiskey stored by Heaven Hill. This could be accounted for later on, since the production sheets were kept in a fire-safe vault. It could have been a huge advertising point for the manufacturer of the vault, but he refrained, probably out of respect for the distillers.

For Heaven Hill it was an enormous disaster. Not only had they lost a considerable amount of maturing whiskey but also they could not produce new spirit. One bright point was that just hours before the fire, the master distiller had made up a batch of the proprietary yeast strain in metal jugs. These were stored in a cooler high up in the distillery and with the help of a crane, the whole cooler was removed after the fire, saving the seven generations old yeast strain. Jim Beam Distillery in Clermont and Early Times Distillery in Louisville offered a temporary solution to making new spirit. Under supervision of Heaven Hill they continued production until the unfortunate distilling company purchased Bernheim Distillery, located in Louisville, in 1999. Since then all Heaven Hill brands have been manufactured there. In recent years the capacity has been doubled and the entire plant has been renovated thoroughly. In Bardstown, Heaven Hill still owns a large number of warehouses, located opposite the Heaven Hill Bourbon Heritage Center, a beautiful museum and visitor's center. Today Heaven Hill is an ultra-modern distillery, owned by the Shapiras, of whom brother Max is in charge. There are still Beams working at the distillery. The current master distillers are father and son Parker and Craig Beam. These days Parker and Craig both keep some of the yeast strain at home, just in case. After all, we can't do without Elijah Craig bourbon.

***

The revered distiller and reverend might have gotten along well with Skip James, had they been living in the same era, since the latter certainly was as multi-talented as Craig. Nehemia Curtis James was born on October 3, 1902, in Bentonia, Mississippi. His father was a preacher after having been an illicit distiller in an earlier career. "Skip" started to play the organ when a teenager and looked like he was going to follow in his father's footsteps. However, when his first wife, who was the daughter of another clergyman, ran away with a World War I veteran, his outlook on life seems to have changed. Skip turned mean and unpredictable, picking up the guitar to become a traveling blues man. He couldn't make a living entirely from playing the blues, so he picked up many other jobs, among which building levees and doing construction work on the roads. He even bootlegged whiskey, returning to his father's old career and unwittingly following Elijah Craig.

In 1931 James was offered a chance to do an audition at H.C. Speir's record shop in Jackson, MS. Speir was impressed. He acted as talent scout and agent for Paramount and arranged for James to travel to their recording studios in Wisconsin. James' record *Devil Got My Woman* might have referred to his first wife leaving him. Various songs indicated that James was still very much influenced by his religious upbringing, like his song "Jesus is a Mighty Good Leader." Unfortunately his records didn't sell well, due in part to the Great Depression. Around 1933 Skip turned to religion. He became a music teacher and joined his father's ministry. Now James set his musical talents to accompany the choir and earned some extra income as a piano tuner. Eventually he was ordained as a minister in various denominations. He didn't record music anymore and virtually disappeared from the blues scene.

If it was not for the great blues revival in the early 1960s we would probably not have known about the man who had been a great influence on his contemporaries Robert Johnson and Son House. Thanks to a couple of serious blues fans who tracked him down in a hospital in Tunica, MS, Skip James reappeared on stage and recorded new material. The 1964 Newport Folk Festival gave him a new lease on his blues life. Thanks to Eric Clapton he even made some extra money on one of his earlier recordings. With his super group The Cream, it was Clapton who turned Skip James' "I Am So Glad" into a hit. Clapton, also musically influenced by Robert Johnson, always credited the original composers of material he covered. The same song was covered a few years later by the English rock group Deep Purple on their debut album *Shades of Deep Purple.*

Skip James continued to enjoy his renewed fame, albeit that he kept warning about the evils surrounding the blues. Clearly he was quite ambivalent about his blues past and his work as a minister. In that respect he differed from Elijah Craig who happily combined his distilling endeavors with preaching the Gospel.

James was not alone in his duality. His contemporary Ishmon Bracey, when rediscovered by zealous blues fans, refused to take the stage again, having become a preacher. Bracey did however help in tracking down Skip James. Another contemporary blues player, the famous slide guitarist Son House, struggled with the same ambivalence and tried his entire life to become a minister, but never succeeded. House was found again in the blues revival of the 1960s, he and James performing at the same festivals for a while, albeit that Son House would profit much longer from his rediscovery. Son House died in 1988, having influenced many later blues musicians, such as Muddy Waters and contemporary rock groups like the Rolling Stones and The White Stripes. The latter group, actually a duo, started to perform in Detroit, where House had retired and would eventually die at the ripe old age of 86.

Skip James died in 1969 but is not forgotten, despite the fact that his old Paramount recordings from 1931 are extremely rare. Luckily most of his work was rerecorded and is still available on CD. In 2000 the Coen Brothers released the movie *O Brother Where Art Thou?* and Skip's song "Hard Time Killing Floor" can be heard on the soundtrack, performed by Chris Thomas King.

Stylistically, Skip James is known for his open D-tuning of the guitar, his three- finger-picking style and his falsetto singing. Some consider him more related to the Piedmont blues than to the Delta blues. Notably, he disliked the folk scene that embraced him in the 1960s. Character-wise he was described as unkind, evasive and distrustful, a man who preferred to play alone and refused to share his talents and abilities with others – a contrast to what is known about Elijah Craig.

Now pour yourself a 12-year-old Elijah Craig, put on The Cream's rendition of "I'm So Glad," sit back, listen, sip and enjoy. It is powerful music with a powerful dram. When satisfied, go for the older stuff and try the 18-year-old with "Devil Got My Woman." A great salute to two great American characters.

A Heaven Hill warehouse at the Bourbon Heritage Center, Bardstown, KY.

Crossroads
Albert Blanton and Robert Johnson

Single cask bottlings have been enjoyed by a select group of Scottish whisky lovers for more than two decades. Today almost every Scottish distillery seems to feel the urge to launch one. This type of whisky is arguably the most original and authentic expression of a distillery, being undiluted and unfiltered before bottling. The bourbon industry appears to have followed in this tradition only recently, presenting various single barrel bourbons to the market. However, that is a misconception. The first commercially available single barrel bourbon was launched in 1984, long before its Scottish siblings mushroomed.

The man responsible in 1984 for the first single barrel bourbon was Elmer T. Lee, a former master distiller at Ancient Age distillery, known as Buffalo Trace since 1999. The distillery is situated in Frankfort, Kentucky at a site where in early times there was a buffalo crossing in the Kentucky River. Lee named his single barrel bourbon Blanton's in honor of Colonel Albert Bacon Blanton. The Colonel started his career at the distillery in 1897 as an office clerk and eventually became co-owner with George T. Stagg, after whom the distillery was named at the time. Blanton developed a preference for the whiskey maturing in one specific warehouse. Instead of the other ones, clad with corrugated iron plates, this one was erected from red-brown brick and known as Warehouse H. The small of stature but dedicated Colonel would make it a habit to regularly select specific casks and have them bottled individually, for special events such as birthdays and for personal use. It proves that single barrel bourbons are more than half a century old, albeit not commercially available at the time.

Colonel Blanton retired in 1952, after having served the distillery for 55 years. His recipes are still in use and besides Blanton's, Buffalo Trace creates various whiskeys from them. Blanton's stopper is world famous. On the cork is a Kentucky racehorse. There are eight different versions and together the stoppers show a horse in full stride. Each horse carries a letter next to its hind leg. The eight different letters together form the word Blantons.

Elmer T. Lee has retired too but can be seen at the distillery sometimes. He incidentally helps with selecting barrels that can be bought by individual customers and bottled according to their wishes. This works as follows. The master distiller chooses five different barrels within the range of the Blanton's flavor profile from Warehouse H and invites the customer to come taste and pick his favorite. A beautiful form of audience participation.

Warehouse H contains approximately 18,000 barrels, stacked three high on four floors. Buffalo Trace has 12 warehouses in total, with a usual stock of 300,000 barrels. The largest one can contain 50,000 and the smallest one only one barrel. Buffalo Trace was the first distillery to cross the threshold of filling the 2nd million barrel after Prohibition and built a special shrine on site for this milestone. It is definitely not only the smallest but also the most expensive warehouse in the industry per liter maturing bourbon. Buffalo Trace is innovative in other areas. It was the first distillery to apply steam heating to the warehouses. Below 40 F the whiskey has little interaction with the wood and in winter the temperature in Kentucky can drop below that point. By heating the warehouses, the whiskey matures at a more rapid pace than would happen in the icy cold. The main reason that bourbon matures so well in Kentucky is the dramatic changes in seasons and temperatures. Various distillers are of the opinion that heated warehouses are not necessary since Mother Nature does the job best.

Buffalo Trace employees are committed to their work. Ronnie Eddins had been working at the distillery for at least three decades when the Kentucky River left its banks in 1997, resulting in the majority of the warehouses being flooded. Eddins quickly chartered a rowboat, setting out for his office to save the administration. He put as many ledgers in the boat as it could carry and moved the rest to the attic of the building. When the water had receded but the buildings still had to be cleaned, he kept his accounts from the back of his car, as long as needed. The floods are an annually recurring worry.

Nonagenarian Jimmy still worked at the place after his 91st birthday and is recorded as the first African American warehouse manager in the history of the distillery. His son Fred used to be an engineer at the site and returned after his retirement to take visitors on tours.

An interesting feature of Buffalo Trace is the barrel

Ferris wheel, lifting the barrels high into the warehouse without backbreaking assistance. It saves time, money and manpower. In contrast with most American distilleries, the yeast strain is not kept alive at the distillery; rather yeast is bought from Red Star of St. Louis, who delivers it freeze-dried. Buffalo Trace uses only one variety to create its entire series of bourbons.

The still house contains a stainless steel column still that can process 60,000 gallons in one run. Even here Buffalo Trace innovates. A recently installed micro still is used to experiment with different distilling regimes and the output is poured in different barrels than your usual virgin white oak. So far we've seen various "wine finishes" on the market, which are interesting as a whiskey but cannot be called bourbon anymore.

Next to the entrance of the distillery terrain stands a stately mansion, Riverside House, being the oldest building in Franklin County, dating from 1775. Before Prohibition it was in use as the company office and after Repeal as a laboratory. Some 15 years ago it had to be closed due to direly needed repairs. All other buildings date after Repeal, although the distillery was one of six possessing a license to sell whiskey to pharmacies for medicinal purposes between 1920 and 1933. This license did not allow them to distill. In 1927 the barrel inventories of bourbon were running low and a temporary permit to distill was granted. Most distilleries were not in operation and the Stitzel distillery in Louisville ran that year to produce bourbon for all six of the license/permit holders. Stitzel distilled bourbon using the grain recipes and yeast cultures of the other distilleries. This production was a sufficient quantity to last to the end of Prohibition.

The visitor center harbors a small museum with a photo display of the resurrection of the distillery. The shop offers whiskey souvenirs and in the adjoining bar visitors can enjoy some of the whiskeys in Buffalo Trace's assortment.

Before Prohibition the distillery was called Old Fire Copper. After that dreadful period it was renamed George T. Stagg, after the then-owner. In the early 1990s lock stock and barrel were sold to the current owner, the Sazerac Family, who changed the name to Buffalo Trace in 1999. In addition to Blanton's, available in four different versions, many different whiskeys are produced here: Buffalo Trace Kentucky Straight Bourbon Whiskey, Eagle Rare Single Barrel, W.L. Weller (a wheated bourbon), Sazerac Rye Kentucky Straight Rye Whisky, Elmer T. Lee's Rye Recipe Kentucky Straight Bourbon, George T. Stagg, Pappy van Winkle's 20-year-old "Wheat Recipe," Thomas H. Handy Rye Whiskey, Rock Hill Farm Single Barrel Bourbon "Rye Recipe," Old Charter, Benchmark, Hancock's Reserve and Ancient Age.

***

With such a versatile, original and innovative distillery as this one it is only logical that a name springs to mind evoking similar qualities in the realm of blues composition and playing: Robert Johnson.

This enigmatic and larger than life blues man was born in Hazlehurst, MS on May 8, 1911, supposedly sold his soul to the devil to learn to play the blues guitar and subsequently died at the young age of 27, on August 16, 1938 in Greenwood, MS, after having been poisoned with strychnine-laced whiskey from an open bottle. A short life, but one with tremendous consequences. Although later research by various blues scholars show that Johnson was largely forgotten soon after his death, he made an indelible stamp on the blues and its influence on rock from 1961 on when early recordings from 1936 and 1937 were released on a landmark album called *King of the Delta Blues Singers*. White blues "investigators" like Alan Lomax and Gayle Wardlow (who would find Johnson's birth certificate many years later), as well as various white jazz enthusiasts, had known how powerful his music was. They were able to track down his half-sister, half-brother and former wife, as well as some musicians who used to play with him and were still alive, among whom Honeyboy Edwards, Robert Lockwood Jr., Johnny Shines and Sonny Boy Williamson II. Due to the research of Lomax, Wardlow and others, early recordings of Johnson were found and his past was pieced together from various interviews. When *King of The Delta Blues Singers* was launched, it ignited a growing interest with aspiring young guitarists like Jimi Hendrix, Eric Clapton, Jimmy Page, Keith Richards and Brian Jones. They started to cover Robert Johnson's songs and this meant a revived worldwide interest in his music. Today many blues musicians still cover Johnson's songs and among them are

"Love in Vain" by the Rolling Stones and "Crossroads" by Eric Clapton. The latter released an entire album to honor the mystical bluesman in 2004, called *Me and Mr. Johnson*.

When biographers started to publish books about Robert Johnson as early as the end of the 1950s, his legend began to grow until it reached almost mythical proportions. Musicians who had traveled and played with him in the 1930s testified of Johnson's incredible style of playing, his versatility and his ability to play any song immediately after he had heard it. However, according to Son House, many years after Johnson's death, the young bluesman couldn't really play well and followed House wherever he could - to learn to play. House supposedly scolded him and sent him away. After two years Johnson reappeared and could play extremely well. It gave birth to the myth that he went to a crossroads in Mississippi to meet the devil and exchange his soul for learning how to play the guitar. House's memory might not have been that clear when he told the story, since it is almost certain he only met Johnson when the latter was already established as a musician. Another spokesman contributes the devil at the crossroads story to guitarist Tommy Johnson, who might have influenced Robert. The devil-myth surrounding his life is also sustained by a story about another Mississippi guitarist called Ike Zinnerman, who taught Robert to play the guitar while sitting on a tombstone. They would practice at midnight at the local cemetery, a fact unveiled by Zinnerman's daughter when interviewed by blues scholar

Bruce Conforth, the first curator of the Rock and Roll Hall of Fame in Cleveland. These are all legends surrounding the phenomenon and it is probable that Robert Johnson cultivated this story himself as a marketing tool. It went down well with the audience to associate blues playing with the devil. Churches condemned the guitar as an instrument of the devil at the time. Bluesman Peetie Wheatstraw for instance advertized himself as the "Devil's son-in-law" and many songs made references to Satan, like "Hellhound on My Trail" and "Me and the Devil. Remarkably enough Johnson's seminal composition "Cross Road Blues" does the opposite and refers to the Almighty instead. The first verse of this song reads:

> "I went to the cross road, fell down on my knees
> I went to the cross road, fell down on my knees
> Asked the Lord above 'Have mercy
> Save poor Bob if you please.'"

The devil at the crossroads legend might also have been a translation error. The ancient African trickster god Papa Legba is a symbol for the spiritual crossroads where access to communication with other worlds can be given or denied. These beliefs were still deeply ingrained in the African American communities in the Delta and obviously such a worldview didn't live well with the Christian faith. African-American preachers might have called Legba the devil due to the lack of a better translation in the English language. Furthermore the singing of secular songs when

91

accompanied by a guitar was seen as a pagan act compared with singing religious chants in the church choir,
where the predominant accompanying musical instrument
was the organ or the piano.

The legend however stuck with Robert Johnson and
helped build his fame long after he had crossed over to
the hereafter. In 1990 Steve Lavere launched a double CD
Box titled *The Complete Recordings*. The set contains 29
recordings of which 12 have alternate takes. The accompanying booklet revealed new facts about Johnson's life. The
term "complete" is not entirely true, since there exists one
other alternate take of "Traveling Riverside Blues," which
was released on another CD than the *King of the Delta Blues
Singers* album. That might have given rise to the theme of
Crossroads, a Hollywood film from 1986 where a young
white blues artist, assisted by an old black musician goes
in search of the "lost" 30th song of Robert Johnson. He
ends up having a guitar contest with the Devil, imperson-
ated by Steve Vai, who also played for the soundtrack of
that movie, together with Ry Cooder. However, the movie
was released four years earlier than LaVere's CD-set. To
put that down as a case of premonition by film director
Walter Hill is tempting when writing about Johnson, but a
bit far-fetched.

Johnson reigned beyond his grave not long after he
died, despite the fact that his companions soon largely
forgot him. Not so with talent scout and record producer John Hammond, who had heard him play in the Delta
once. When the latter organized his famous Carnegie Hall

From Spirituals to Swing concert on December 23, 1938 he wanted to bill Robert Johnson and then found out he had already passed away. Instead Hammond booked Big Bill Broonzy, but as a morbid support act to posthumously honor the highly creative and versatile guitarist, first played two of Johnson's recordings: "Walking Blues" and "Preaching Blues." The audience listened in awe to a dead man perform.

When listening to Robert Johnson's song the ear will pick out the different styles that come with each track. Johnson was known to please his audience by playing any style they wanted, from country via gospel to blues and even jazz, as can be heard on the track "Red Top." Johnson also recorded three-minute well-rounded compositions and could repeat them almost perfectly for a second take. This was in sharp contrast with most of his contemporaries who would start to play, not paying much attention to meter and often running out of time at the end of the recording, limited to three minutes for technical reasons, resulting in a rushed, unpolished ending. It is not overstated to say that Robert Johnson was the first recorded blues man who took the "cottage industry style" of the individual musician to a commercial, but still unique level. A comparison comes to mind with Elmer T. Lee's launch of the first commercially available single barrel bourbon - Blanton's, matured under the watchful eye of the warehouse men in the distillery where it is crafted.

It may well be true that Johnson has become a greater influence on modern rock groups than he ever was on his contemporaries. His ability to charm the female portion of his audience and go home with one of them in each town where he performed fits the pattern of groupies surrounding the big rock acts of the latter part of the 20th century. This influence on rock is best epitomized by Led Zeppelin's lead singer Robert Plant who reportedly said in 2004, "Robert Johnson, to whom we all owed our existence, in some way."

Robert Johnson certainly stood at a crossroads where the less structured style of songsters like Blind Lemon Jefferson, Son House and Charlie Patton met with a more commercial approach to the blues. That crossroads has been bridged, like the buffalos at Blanton's distillery once forded the Kentucky River.

In Johnson's words, "The blues is a low-down, aching chill; If you ain't never had 'em, I hope you never will."

Well, if you had 'em, then warm your spirit with one of the five Blanton expressions while listening to "Walking Blues" or "Cross Road Blues."

Barrels for Blanton's cross the road at Buffalo Trace.

Slippin' and Slidin'
Bill Samuels and Memphis Slim

About four miles southeast of the tiny village of Loretto, Kentucky is Hardin's Creek, the place where Mr. Charles Burks built a mill and a distillery in 1805. After his demise in 1831, the distillery stayed in the family. His grandson George started working for the firm in 1878, thoroughly renovated the distillery and added a farm and a bottling plant. He named the complex "Burks Spring" and contracted John C. Weller, a distributor from Louisville in 1906. Business remained successful until 1920, when the distillery was forced to close due to National Prohibition.

Burks decided to sell lock, stock and barrel to Mr. Ernest Bickett, whose primary interest was the farm. The barrels with whiskey mysteriously disappeared from the warehouse, due to a certain George Remus, a shady lawyer and bootlegger who originated from Germany. He discovered a loophole in the Volstead Act that enabled Prohibition: if he bought a distillery and a pharmacy he could sell liquor to himself for medicinal purposes. Subsequently he hijacked his own stash and put it on the black market. Remus is said to have made over $40 million within three years. Eventually the cunning lawyer was caught and hit the blues with a two-year sentence in the Atlanta Federal Penitentiary for bootlegging. His wife Imogene then began an affair with Frank Dodge, a Prohibition agent. Together they stripped Remus of his assets and even tried to have him killed by a hired gun. In 1927 Remus was taken to court in Cincinnati to finalize the divorce that Imogene had demanded. When he spotted the cab of his wife and daughter he chased their cart through Eden Park, cornered them and shot Imogene. She died the same day. When put to trial Remus defended himself and pled temporary insanity. He was sentenced to an asylum for six months. After his release he tried to get back into bootlegging but gave up when he found out the business was taken over by an infamous group of gangsters. Remus then moved back to Kentucky where he led a further unremarkable life and died twenty years after the end of Prohibition.

Immediately after Repeal, Bickett's sons Orris and Frank resurfaced and picked up distilling again. Ten years later, in 1943, they sold their rebuilt whiskey business to Glenmore. The new owner was not only interested in the stocks of matured whiskey, but also landscaped a beautiful large lake in the hills nearby. A pipeline supplied cooling water from the lake to the distillery. Soon after World War II the distillery was acquired by Mr. D.W. Karp who produced whiskey at the site until 1951. The buildings remained empty for a couple of years, until T.W. "Bill" Samuels emerged and bought the neglected complex.

Bill Samuels was no stranger to the whiskey business. His great-great-great-grandfather Robert Samuels was registered as a licensed distiller in Pennsylvania as early as 1779. He probably took his still with him when he moved to Kentucky in 1780. Great-great-grandfather William ran a tiny operation, but great-grandfather Taylor William

Samuels had his distillery officially registered in 1844 and created a commercial success with Old Samuel's Whiskey. He was the largest landowner around and elected High Sheriff four times. In 1866 the fourth generation, grandfather William Isaac, took over the management. When he died in 1898, father Leslie took over and he had to stop production in 1920, like so many other distillers. He continued the business in 1933, reorganized and built up a new distillery that passed into the hands of his son Bill. In 1943 Bill retired and sold T.W. Samuels Distillery to Country Distillers.

Some 10 years later Bill was back in business when he purchased the old Burks Distillery ruins at Loretto. With great care, love and a sense of history Bill started a restoration project that was finished in early 1954. He baptized the complex Star Hill Distillery, after the family farm in Bardstown. In its first year Star Hill produced 1,527 barrels of excellent whiskey, made with a mash bill that significantly differs from most bourbon mash bills. Samuels did not use rye as a flavor grain, but rather wheat. He also managed to keep his own yeast strain alive. It survived Prohibition and it is generally accepted that this strain is the oldest in the American whiskey industry.

The distillery slowly grew into a stable position. The seventh generation of Samuels, Bill Jr., was already working at the distillery when Hiram Walker & Sons purchased Star Hill in 1981. In the late 1990s the distillery changed hands again. Allied Lyons acquired it, but maintained Bill Samuels, Jr. as President. If it ain't broke, don't fix it, they must have thought. Today Bill Jr. is still responsible for the quality of the end product: a straight wheated bourbon. The current owner is Fortune Brands, who puts the distillery in the capable hands of its drinks subsidiary Beam Global.

The Samuels family sold Old Samuel's whiskey as early as 1780, whereas Charles Burks launched a nameless whiskey in 1805. His grandson George introduced the brands Burks Spring and Old Happy Hollow. Distributor John C. Weller later added the brands Faymus and J.C.W. When Bill Samuels, Sr. eventually purchased the neglected distillery in 1953 and restarted production after the necessary restoration, he decided to call the whiskey Old Samuel's again. This raised a problem at the Foster Trading Company, who at that time had purchased Bill's old family distillery from Country Distillers. Foster went to court and after a couple of years won the legal battle. Bill Sr. was not allowed to use his own name for the whiskey he so proudly produced. Bill owned another brand name, Star Hill, the same name he used for the distillery itself. So why shouldn't he apply it to the whiskey as well?

In 1957 George Shields, general manager of an advertising company and frequent visitor to Bill's distillery presented a totally new promotion campaign, including the name Maker's Mark. Whether he came up with that name himself is not certain. According to the Samuels family, Bill Sr.'s wife Margie was responsible for it. She collected fine pewter and knew each piece bore the sign of its maker. Such a mark was synonymous with quality and the same could be said of her husband's whiskey. Margie is also supposed to have introduced the habit of dipping each bottle in hot red wax to seal it off and prevent tampering with the contents. (Remember what happened to Robert Johnson?) It is romantic enough to be held for the truth and this story is sustained by a whole army of "dippin' ladies" working in the bottling plant. It all contributes to the myth of Maker's Mark.

With a Samuels at the helm, a very distinct bourbon has been created here since 1953. Not only the taste emphasizes that fact, but also the way in which the whiskey is produced. Bill Samuels, Sr. was preoccupied with quality control and had outspoken opinions about how whiskey should be made. He watched every detail. As a result of his manic behavior regarding the quality of the product, the production costs of Maker's Mark are significantly higher, compared to most other Kentucky bourbons. Everything is done at the site, even the manufacturing of the labels. For that purpose at the distillery premises stands a little print shop. The labels are hand-printed and die cut here. The design is from the hand of Bill Samuels, Sr. and worthwhile looking at. It has an interesting story. The circle with star under the "M" refers to Star Hill Farm, the grounds on which the distillery stands. The "S" is for Samuels and the "IV" for the 4th generation. At the time Bill Sr. assumed that his great-grandfather started distilling. Bill Jr. later delved into the family archives and found out that his father must have mistaken himself two generations. "But he was a dyslectic as well," joked Bill Jr. once, when interviewed. If that is true, Bill Sr. wasn't historically incorrect but instead saw the "VI" for an "IV" when proofreading the print.

The Maker's Mark mash bill is 70% corn, 16% wheat, and 14% malted barley. The corn and wheat are not genetically modified and come from the south of Indiana and from Kentucky. The malted barley is transported to the distillery from Milwaukee, Wisconsin. The standard Maker's Mark bottling is 90 proof (45% ABV). For the Kentucky Derby a special Mint Julep whiskey is packaged in the distinctive bottle, sporting green wax on the neck.

Close to the entrance stands the Quart House, a retail shop from 1889, where the farmers used to go to have their flasks and bottles re-filled, straight from the barrel. This monument is said to be the oldest surviving liquor store in the US, albeit that no whiskey is sold there anymore. The distillery is designated as a National Historic Landmark. Its site is idyllic; the whiskey made here is one of the mellowest bourbons from Kentucky.

***

As the name suggests, Memphis Slim came from that temple of music in Tennessee, where he was born on September 3, 1915 as John Len Chatman. Having been influenced by his father who not only played guitar and piano, but also sang and ran various juke joints, he was destined for a career in the blues. Multi-talented and a stickler for detail, wanting to do everything himself - just like the

Samuels at Maker's Mark. He developed over the years as an accomplished composer and bandleader. He made more than 500 recordings before he died in Paris, France in 1988, a lauded musician.

The road to fame wasn't easy at first. In the 1930s Chatman played the circuit of dance halls, gambling places, honky-tonk bars and juke joints, probably helped by his father. He didn't travel far, mainly playing in West Memphis, Arkansas and the southeastern part of Missouri. When he moved to Chicago at the turn of the 1930s he had learned the hard life on the road as a solo player. In the windy city he decided to form a duo with guitarist and singer Big Bill Broonzy. Together they began to hit the club circuit. In 1940/41 he recorded his first songs with the Bluebird Label under the name Memphis Slim, given to him by the record producer Lester Melrose. The latter offered him a place as a session musician in the studio, a job that gave him the opportunity to accompany many blues players who would become famous in their own right.

Around 1946 Slim presented himself increasingly as a band leader, riding piggyback on the emergence of Louis Jordan's Jump Blues, which constituted combos containing piano, upright bass, drums, guitar and saxophones. He also recorded with trios and quartets and met famous bass player, composer and arranger Willie Dixon. They formed a band called Slim and the House Rockers, which rapidly became a moneymaker for them. They even managed to get a number one hit in the R&B charts. Soon they were touring in a greater area. Meanwhile Slim continued recording records with various labels. From that period stems probably his most famous song "Nobody Loves Me," in the future to be covered as "Every Day I Have the Blues" by numerous artists among whom Ray Charles, B.B. King, Eric Clapton, Carlos Santana and Jimi Hendrix.

Although Memphis Slim was now slippin' and slidin' through the world of blues related music, he experienced some financial difficulties when his record label went out of business in the early 1950s. When various other companies picked him up in the decade that followed he was able to continue his steady stream of recordings. One of his new sidemen became Matt "Guitar" Murphy, who would feature years later in *The Blues Brothers* starring John Belushi and Dan Aykroyd.

In 1960 Willie Dixon took Memphis Slim on a two year tour of Europe where the latter discovered a suave way of living he liked so much that he moved to Paris, France permanently. The young boy that used to play in juke joints and gambling halls was now a revered American blues musician in the Old World. Memphis Slim was a talented storyteller and presenter with a pleasant demeanor and a great sense of humor. Soon he was in demand all over Europe and established himself as one of the most important blues musicians of the 1970s and 1980s. Television became more common in households and Slim began to appear on TV in many European countries. He was also invited to play a role in various French movies and even wrote the score for one.

His style of playing was as versatile as his switching

between solo performances and groups and his humor must have matched that of Bill Samuels, Jr. It not only shone through in the way he presented his songs, but also in his texts and titles that often had double entendres, a characteristic of many blues songs. Slim's song about a woman who ran away, titled "If You See Kay," leaves little to the imagination regarding what he really meant to say! He always honored the man who influenced his playing the piano: Leroy Carr, a very talented blues singer, pianist and songwriter from Memphis, TN, who died in 1935 at only 30 years old. Carr is said to have been killed by nephritis, which is plausible because Carr was a severe alcoholic. His "How Long, How Long Blues," recorded in 1928, became an instant classic and has since been covered by many musicians throughout the world.

The French clearly loved Memphis Slim. In 1986 he was rewarded with the title "Commandeur dans l'Ordre des Arts et des Lettres" by the Ministry of Culture of the French Republic. His homeland didn't forget him either, making him Ambassador-at-Large of Good Will. When he died in Paris, his remains were flown back to the USA and buried at Galilee Memorial Gardens in Memphis, Tennessee. A year later he would be honored posthumously by being inducted into the Blues Hall of Fame.

Memphis Slim's legacy lives on in the huge number of songs he wrote, still being played by many musicians today. He sure left his mark behind in the world of the blues. Let's enjoy his smooth and entertaining blues while sippin' a mellow wheated bourbon that leaves its own distinctive mark.

The Whisky Creek crosses the grounds of Maker's Mark.

Hey, Bartender
Jim Beam and Koko Taylor

Distilleries have changed hands time and again. It happens all over the world. But there is one big difference between Scotland and the USA. Some Scottish distilleries are still in the hands of descendants from the original founding family. Alas, that cannot be said about American distilleries. Prohibition wreaked havoc on the American whiskey industry and many distilling dynasties were destroyed. Only a handful emerged from the Noble Experiment and today only seven or eight distilleries survive, the micro-distilleries that have become *en vogue* since the mid-1990s excluded. Among them they make nearly 100 different bourbons and American whiskeys. In some cases however there are still slender ties with the original families and even between both whisky-making nations...

It is generally acknowledged that the Irish invented whiskey making and the Scots are credited for marketing the drink worldwide. As mentioned in a previous chapter, European immigrants took their distilling habits with them when they crossed the Atlantic. In the last quarter of the 18th century many a Scottish, German, Irish or Dutch craftsman set sail to prove his luck in the Land of Unlimited Possibilities. One of them was a German named Johannes Jacob Bohm, who started distilling whiskey around 1785. For convenience he changed his name to Beam and unknowingly became the founding father of today's bestselling bourbon worldwide. The first whiskey he sold was known as Old Jake Beam Sour Mash. David Beam, the founder's 10th child, took over the Beam family distillery, the farm and the gristmill in 1820, at the age of 18. At first the distillery was named Old Tub. In 1857 Old Tub distillery was relocated just north of Bardstown in Nelson County, Kentucky by David M. Beam, grandson of Jacob Beam. He did this to take advantage of the then-latest in transport: railway. Old Tub whiskey, which sold for 25 cents a gallon in prewar-1860, could sell for up to $35 a gallon in wartime. No wonder David M. Beam continued to distill whiskey as long as possible during the Civil War.

When Jacob's grandson Jim "Beauregard" Beam took over the company he changed the name to Clear Creek Distillery. He then purchased a second distillery to increase capacity. Around 1920 he had to close them both and sell Clear Creek, thanks to Prohibition. During those 13 long years, Jim Beam tried to run three different companies, all failures: the Sunlight Mining Company, the Sunbeam Quarries Company and a citrus grove in Florida. At the end of the Noble Experiment he said to his children and nephews "Boys, time for us to get back to work." The current Jim Beam distillery in Clermont, Kentucky was built in 120 days in 1934. Think somebody was in a hurry to get re-started?

Jim Beam now began producing Colonel James B. Beam bourbon since he had sold the brand Old Tub along with Clear Creek Distillery. By the late 1930s, the bourbon was known as Jim Beam Kentucky Straight Bourbon Whiskey.

Jim had also developed a new culture of yeast for his freshly built distillery. He was so protective of his bourbon's yeast strain, every Friday night (even after he retired in 1944) he took a sealed jar of it home – strapped into the passenger seat of his Cadillac. That car was his trademark and he owned a whole string of them over his lifetime. Jim Beam's son, T. Jeremiah Beam once failed to make a reporter understand in technical terms the importance of the family yeast strain. After a lot of explaining he looked at the uncomprehending person who interviewed him and stated, "Let's just say we think it makes a better bourbon." The same yeast strain is used today.

When Jim Beam lent his name to the whiskey, the sales figures literally beamed off the page. To honor this legendary whiskey baron the well-known square bottle still bears his signature, blown in the glass. The sixth generation of descendants included Booker Noe, probably one of the greatest legends in the contemporary American whiskey industry. Booker traveled the world to spread the word about Jim Beam and its small batch bourbons. He had the habit of taking a small number of barrels from the middle of his warehouses and bottling the whiskey directly, not diluted or filtered. It was his own private stock and he called it Booker's Bourbon. This was the rise of four small batch bourbons produced by Jim Beam. The other ones are Baker's, Basil Hayden and Knob Creek. When Booker died on February 24, 2004, he was soon immortalized on the distillery grounds with a bronze statue. Every day, rain or shine, Booker looks over the distillery, sitting in his favorite rocking chair while a statuette of his loyal dog, who only survived him a couple of weeks, keeps him company.

The current owner is Fortune Brands, who has consolidated all its drinks companies under the name Beam Global. At the helm of Jim Beam stands Booker's son Fred Noe, the seventh generation direct descendant of Jacob Bohm. With Jim Beam being the best selling bourbon worldwide, you wouldn't miss it behind any bar from Alaska to Zimbabwe easily. Hey Bartender, pour me one!

A closer look at Beam's portfolio of drinks reveals the presence of another bourbon, Maker's Mark, and a couple of Scottish cousins, most notably the famous blend Teacher's and the pungent, iodine-flavored Islay single malt Laphroaig that has a large following world-wide.

Laphroaig was founded by two brothers in the first quarter of the 19th century: Donald and Alexander Johnston. The former one being the more entrepreneurial of the two bought his brother's shares in 1836. Donald died in 1846 after having fallen in a vat of "burnt ale", a residue from the pot still. He left the distillery to his son Dugald who had to go to court with his sisters. They disputed his heritage. Dugald won, but having no heir, left Laphroaig to his sister Isabella who happened to be married with her cousin, another Alexander Johnston.

For two more generations descendants of Donald Johnston owned the distillery. The last Johnston-related owner never married, died childless in 1954 and left the distillery to his secretary Bessie Williamson. And under this remarkable woman's leadership - she was chosen Woman of The Year in the 1950's in the UK - the USA and Scotland met for the first time regarding the history and ownership of Laphroaig.

Between 1963 and 1972 Bessie sold her shares in three chunks to Long John International, owned by Seager and Evans, ultimately owned by the American Schenley Corporation, one of the whisky companies that rose from the ashes of Prohibition. Bessie stayed on the Board and was "used" as a marketing tool in the USA to promote Scottish whisky. She made many transatlantic travels before retiring in 1973.

This American-Scottish marriage lasted until 1975 when UK brewer Whitbread acquired Long John and with it Laphroaig. The Islay whisky didn't really prosper in their hands and they eventually decided to focus on their primary market and expertise: beer. Laphroaig had to be sold and changed hands again in 1989, becoming part of Allied Lyons, renamed Allied Domecq in 1994 after the merger with the Spanish drinks company. That merger coincided with the appointment of a new manager who would become a legend in his own right: Iain Henderson, aka Mr. Laphroaig. This down-to-earth humor-loving Scot knew his history and set out to put Laphroaig on the map again. Like Bessie Williamson he started to travel internationally and personally promote the whisky he crafted with so much care. In 1994 he launched The Friends of Laphroaig, which turned out to be one of the most successful loyalty programs ever, with the eponymous website as its main driving force.

Today there are more than 270,000 Friends worldwide. They each "own" one square foot on the distillery grounds and are allowed to put their (paper) national flag on it. From every corner of the world Friends travel to Islay, collect their "rent" in the form of a miniature bottle of 10-year-old Laphroaig and perform rituals on their square foot of Islay peat bog. Marriage proposals and dispersing of the ashes of beloved ones are not uncommon among them.

Henderson retired in 2002, thus not witnessing a renewed marriage between Scotland and the USA. In 2006 Allied Domecq sold Laphroaig to Fortune Brands who added the single malt to its drinks portfolio. The honeymoon is over, but a famous movie line could easily be turned into a new marketing slogan: "Beam me up, Scotty!" Today the Scottish heritage in the American whiskey industry is still firmly grounded.

Jim Beam repackages and distributes its Scottish brothers Laphroaig and Teacher's throughout the USA. And 90% of Laphroaig's whisky is quietly maturing in ex-bourbon casks!

***

Where Jim Beam might be called the King of Bourbon, Koko Taylor decidedly earned her nickname Queen of the Blues. There are more comparisons to be made here. Beam is a long lasting family affair with Beams still working at various places in the whiskey industry. Koko Taylor started to play the blues at an early age with her five siblings. They accompanied themselves on homemade instruments. That was in the early 1930s, probably shortly after Prohibition, when Beam made its comeback on the whiskey stage and eventually became the No 1 bourbon in the world, having won many prizes underway. Taylor in her turn would eventually become the most lauded blues woman in the world, having her own Koko Taylor Day in Chicago when on March 3, 1993 then mayor Richard Daley decided to honor its famous citizen in this special way.

Cora Walton, Koko's given name, left her hometown in Tennessee in 1952 at the age of 24, to travel with Robert "Pops" Taylor to Chicago and try her luck in the local blues clubs. She would later marry him and share successes with him onstage, taking his surname, but when they arrived in Chicago, according to her they had nothing but "thirty-five cents and a box of Ritz crackers."

At first the big city wasn't easy on them. Taylor had a job at a packaging company and the future Queen of the Blues kept herself employed by cleaning houses. When they had time they would listen to blues acts in the evening and Koko was encouraged by her husband to sit in with some bands. It didn't take long before she enjoyed guest appearances everywhere. In 1962, exactly ten years after they left Tennessee, Koko was introduced to Chess Records by already famous Willie Dixon. This great blues-man – great by composure and great by creativity - rear-ranged "Wang Dang Doodle" for Koko in 1965. This was a song he had originally composed in 1960 and recorded with Howlin' Wolf. It turned out to be an incredible hit and sold over a million copies. Koko's star was rising and when she switched record companies in 1975, teaming up with Bruce Iglauer's Alligator Records, it was only for the better.

For Iglauer it wasn't the first Taylor in his group, as he had been recording Hound Dog Taylor since 1971, having fallen in love with the guitarist's music. At the turn of the 1960s Iglauer was a shipping clerk at Delmark Records and tried to interest his boss in recording Hound Dog but the former refused. The young clerk didn't take no for answer, left Delmark and started his own record company. His first release was *Hound Dog Taylor and The Rockers*. Hound Dog, who could regularly be seen and heard playing at Chicago's open air Maxwell Street Market, was well known in the scene for his slide guitar playing but also for a rather remarkable physical attribute: his left hand had six fingers! Hound Dog Taylor died in 1975. As far as is known these two Taylors were not related.

Koko Taylor's Alligator years brought her world fame and after her first album in 1975, eight more would follow, the last being released in 2007. All but one received a Grammy Nomination. She toured the world for decades with various famous blues and rock musicians, among whom B.B. King, Buddy Guy, Muddy Waters and Led Zeppelin's Robert Plant & Jimmy Page. She appeared in *Wild at Heart*, a David Lynch film from 1990, next to Nicolas Cage and Laura Dern; and in the sequel *Blues Brothers 2000*, with Aretha Franklin, Matt Murphy and a score of blues musicians in it.

Koko, this nickname given to her because of her fondness for chocolate, has probably won more awards than any other blues musician – with the exception of B.B. King - but also had her blues. She almost died in a car crash in 1989, but managed to come back after recovery. Her attempt to run her own blues club in Chicago was a short-lived adventure. After the opening in 1994, it closed a mere 5 years later. Well into her seventies she continued to play many concerts yearly, apparently earning good money, since she ran into some trouble with the Internal Revenue Service who claimed in 2008 that Taylor owed them more than $400,000 in back taxes and the subsequent interest and fines.

On June 3, 2009 the Queen of the Blues died in a hospital of complications from surgery. Not even four weeks earlier she had given her last performance at the Blues Music Awards Ceremony, where she received the award for Traditional Blues Female Artist of the Year. Taylor's style was traditional indeed. She had a rough, powerful voice. While listening to local radio stations when still young, she might have been influenced by earlier female blues singers, most notably Ma Rainey (The Mother of The Blues) and Bessie Smith (The Empress of The Blues). The former successfully performed "Booze 'n' Blues" with a small orchestra and the latter sang about bootleg liquor in "Nobody Knows You When You're Down and Out," both candidates for teaming up with bourbon. Rainey and Smith however had a hard and fast life, both dying relatively young, whereas Koko Taylor lived to the age of 80. She influenced many female blues musicians such as Bonnie Raitt, Janis Joplin, Susan Tedeschi and Rory Block, the latter being famous for her number "Lovin' Whisky."

In hindsight we can say that "Wang Dang Doodle" was not only the song that started Koko Taylor's success, but it also became her swan song at the Awards Ceremony. However, another favorite of hers was the Floyd Dixon jump blues song "Hey Bartender." Let's order a shot of Jim Beam Black to honor the Queen.

Statue of whiskey icon Booker Noe.

Jim Beam Distillery in Clermont, Kentucky.

Mr. President
George Washington and Gatemouth Brown

"Distillery is a business I am entirely unacquainted with, but from your knowledge of it and from the confidence you have in the profit to be derived from the establishment, I am disposed to enter upon one." Thus wrote George Washington to his plantation manager James Anderson in June 1797.

Anderson came from Scotland and that says it all. Being a farmer looking for a more prosperous life he emigrated from Inverkeithing and took his distilling knowledge with him. With the consent of his employer he set to work immediately. It wasn't long before Washington could profit from the Scot's knowledge and zeal. Only two years later five pot stills at Mount Vernon Estate produced 11,000 gallons, making a profit of $7,500 - a small fortune at the time.

George Washington kept a diary and was a fervent letter writer. Thanks to those characteristics many facts are known about his life, work and way of thinking. He was born on February 22, 1732, on his father's plantation in Pope's Creek, Westmoreland County, Virginia. Age three he moved with his parents and siblings to Little Hunting Creek Plantation, later to be known as Mount Vernon. When 11 he lost his father and George was unable to enjoy a formal education in England as his brothers had done. In 1748 he became a surveyor thanks to the help of an influential Fairfax family, in-laws of his half-brother Lawrence. When Lawrence died in 1752, he left Mount Vernon to George, as well as his place in the Virginia Militia. Soon George would be involved in the conflicts with the French. He became so successful as a soldier that he was appointed supreme commander of the Virginian army in 1755. When peace returned four years later he married a wealthy widow and withdrew from public and military life to his plantation. There he lived and enjoyed the life of the landed gentry for many years. Then he became politically active, earning a seat in the Continental Congress in 1774. When the Revolutionary War started in 1776 his peaceful life came to an abrupt end. Washington returned to the army and after five years of uninterrupted fighting with the English he accepted commander Cornwallis' surrender of the British Army on October 19, 1781. He returned to his beloved Mount Vernon, but stayed politically active. In 1785 he was instrumental in establishing the American Constitution. When it passed in 1787, for the first time in history presidential elections were held in the young Federation. Washington won all votes unanimously, a fact that until today has not been repeated by any other American president. He served two terms from 1789 till 1797, after which time he returned to Mount Vernon again, where he learned to distill at the age of 65.

Although not a heavy imbiber himself, he was a big proponent of whiskey for the army. In 1777 he instructed the procurement officer of the Continental Army "there should always be enough whiskey to give moderate portions to the troops...especially when they have to march in hot or cold weather, and have to make their camp in the wet cold...it is so essential that we cannot do without."

Washington was not only a successful military commander and politician, but also a sound businessman and seemingly enlightened landowner. He educated his slaves in various professions, such as shoemaker, blacksmith, mason and distiller, with the intention that when the slaves were free men, they could earn a living. As a politician he once learned a valuable lesson about whiskey. In the middle of the 18th century it was not unusual to "buy" votes by offering free whiskey to the common people just before the elections started. Only once Washington did not comply with that custom and he immediately lost. It wouldn't happen to him a second time. Whiskey would now earn votes and money.

Unfortunately he only enjoyed his new venture for two years. On December 14, 1799 the first President of the United States died of pneumonia. His last words were, "I die hard, but I am not afraid to go."

The distillery was kept alive albeit not easily. Washington's nephew Lawrence Lewis was named the official heir. James Anderson left the estate and that must have been a severe loss to the new owner. In 1808 the stills were fired for the last time. The buildings were not maintained and in 1814 they burnt to the ground. It seemed to be the definitive end of Mount Vernon Distillery. Or not.

181 years later a small miracle happened. In 1995 the possible resurrection of the 18th century distillery was

investigated. Between 1997 and 1998 the entire location was charted thoroughly and from 1999 to 2002 exhaustive excavations took place. It took considerable time to get the necessary permits, but in 2005 the rebuilding started, thanks to a 1.2 million dollar donation of the Distilled Spirits Council of the US (DISCUS). On September 27, 2006 the distillery was reopened by HRH Prince Andrew. A DISCUS spokesman remarked at the occasion, "This is an incredible possibility for America to restore the heritage of distillation, lost during Prohibition."

Today the distillery is part of Mount Vernon Estate, which boasts a few million visitors per year. They all want to see the home of George Washington with their own eyes. DISCUS uses Mount Vernon as the starting place of the American Whiskey Trail. For the opening festivities a small amount of whiskey was distilled following the recipe that could have been used by Washington and Anderson two centuries ago. The copper pot still is an exact replica of a 200-year-old still that was found and confiscated by the police after a moonshine raid. The manufacturing year on the still reads 1787 but it is unclear whether it was ever used by the President or his Scottish manager.

The entirely reconstructed distillery is the only one in the USA that shows from start to finish how whiskey would have been made in the 18th century. Beside the stone and wooden still house one can see Washington's old water mill, also restored to its former splendor. It supplies the distillery with milled grain. Whiskey is only made in small quantities for special events. The still man dresses in traditional clothing and the whiskey is only sold on the premises. The barrels for aging are copies of 19th century 10-gallon casks. So President Washington not only is remembered daily with his portrait on the dollar bill, but also reclaims his rightful position in American whiskey history.

***

Someone who had something to say about the dollar bill in the realm of the blues was Clarence "Gatemouth" Brown. Apart from that, as a person he was at least as talented and versatile as the first President of the United States. Born in Louisiana in 1924 but brought up in Texas, where he would eventually die in 2005, Brown got his nickname from his high school teacher, who reportedly told him he had a "voice like a gate." He was 21 when his professional musical career took off. He first played the drums, but rapidly developed himself as an excellent multi-instrumentalist, mastering guitar, mandolin, piano, harmonica, violin, viola and, not surprisingly given his nickname, vocals. Although a blues man first, he embraced other styles and as easily played Cajun, swing, jazz, and country music. He is said to be one of the first electric guitar players who made use of the capodastro, a device to shorten the strings and raise the pitch.

In 1947 Gatemouth Brown got a big chance in a famous Houston nightclub one evening when house musician and well-known guitarist T-Bone Walker fell ill. Walker was almost 14 years Brown's senior and an excellent guitarist, an inspiration for generations of guitar players to come. His "Stormy Monday" has been covered by many bands and in the 1960s blues revival, Walker teamed up with Memphis Slim and Willie Dixon, performing at the 1962 American Folk Blues Festival.

That particular night in the Houston club, Gatemouth knew whose shoes he had to fill. He took the stand and became famous overnight. The owner of the night club was so impressed by his brilliant guitar playing that he started a record company two years later, to capture Gatemouth's guitar playing for posterity.

For a decade the two would collaborate and launch albums under the label Peacock Records. Then Gatemouth apparently wanted to move on and traveled to Nashville, Tennessee where he soon appeared in various television shows. For a while he had enough of the music industry and moved to New Mexico, where he found a job as a deputy sheriff. When young European guitarists began to explore the roots of the blues more deeply in England and various other countries, Gatemouth Brown was soon re-discovered and persuaded to leave his post of justice to return to the stage. His talent and his popularity as a multi-instrumentalist spread and he toured Europe numerous times in the 1970s, including performances at the renowned Montreux Jazz Festival. The US State Department also honored him, officially appointing Gatemouth as Ambassador for American Music.

The US recording industry took a renewed interest in Brown and in the 1980s various records were launched, for instance with Alligator Records and Verve. He started touring again and managed to perform nearly 300 shows a year. Many awards followed, among which eight W.C. Handy awards, a Grammy for his album *Alright Again!*, and the National Academy of Recording Arts and Sciences Heroes Award. His induction into the Blues Foundation Hall of Fame came in 1999.

Brown was politically engaged, no doubt about that, as can be heard in "Dollar Got the Blues." He also put his money where his mouth was, touring in countries with unstable governments and politically difficult circumstances, saying "People can't come to me, so I go to them." What followed were tours in Africa, the then-Soviet Union and Central America.

Many famous musicians referred to Gatemouth Brown as a big influence on their own music, such as Albert Collins, Jonny Guitar Watson, JJ Cale and even Frank Zappa who claimed that the multi-instrumentalist was his favorite guitar player.

In the fall of 2004 his health deteriorated rapidly. At the time he was living in Slidell, Louisiana. Sadly his house was destroyed by Hurricane Katrina in 2005 and he returned to Orange, Texas where he grew up. Thus, at the end of his life it seemed to be "Stormy Monday" again. In his childhood home he died on September 10, having reached the age of 81, and was buried in the local cemetery. It seemed T-Bone Walker's song came down to haunt him even after his death, since the 2008 Hurricane Ike conjured up a flooding that severely damaged Gatemouth's grave. Fortunately his recordings cannot be washed away.

What to sip while listening to "Dollar Bill got the Blues"? That's a difficult one. Mount Vernon whiskey is hard to get and there's not much available anyway. If you can't get to a bottle of George Washington's whiskey, try another presidential whiskey: Jefferson's Reserve Straight Bourbon Whiskey or, when you really want to pay a tribute to Gatemouth Brown, get hold of a bottle of Sam Houston, a bourbon named after the first president of the Republic of Texas, the state where Brown spent so much of his life.

One Bourbon, One Scotch and One Bird
Jimmy Russell and John Lee Hooker

Almost all American whiskey distilleries have a checkered history due to the numerous takeovers and mergers, reconstructions, rebuilding after severe fires and, last but not least, that wretched Prohibition. For 13 years most US distilleries were silent, except the handful that was granted a license to sell whiskey "for medicinal purposes." Wild Turkey was not one of them. Wild Turkey didn't even exist as a brand at that time, albeit that this characteristically spicy bourbon has been produced since 1868. How did that happen?

1868 signposted the birth of a distillery that only acquired its name "Wild Turkey" in 2001. In the second half of the 19th century, a threesome of businessmen from Anderson County, Kentucky financed the founding of Walker, Martin & Co Distillery in Tyrone, a little town in a bend of the Kentucky River. About one year later, Monroe Walker, Sam Martin and James Ripy sold the distillery to Ripy's son T.B. and Judge W.H. McBrayer. After another year the judge bailed out and in 1870 T.B. Ripy was the proud, sole owner. Soon he was respected for his excellent whiskies and decided to expand the business. By 1880 he had relocated and expanded the distillery no less than five times. In 1885 T.B. bought Old Joe Distillery. After a few years he sold Old Joe, but maintained five warehouses opposite the distillery.

A little bit further up the road, also on the border of the Kentucky River, was another distillery, built by J.W. Stevens. It was sold to J.P. Ripy, a brother of T.B., in 1888. After a thorough renovation he renamed Stevens' distillery Old Hickory Springs. Four years later the Ripy brothers merged. In 1909 they became part of the Kentucky Distillers and Warehouse Corp. T.B.'s sons, still connected to the distillery, bought two other distilleries in 1905 and 1911, respectively D.L. Moore and - again - Old Joe.

All of these distilleries closed due to Prohibition. With repeal, the heirs of Ripy reorganized, concentrated and renovated, after which they resumed making whiskey at the site of the former D.L. Moore distillery. A short while after reopening the distillery, the Ripy family sold out to Bob Gould, who named the plant J.T.S. Brown. One of the Ripys remained, occupying a seat on the board of the new company. In 1972 the respected drinks merchant and distributor Austin Nichols (founded in 1855) took over the distillery and kept Ernie Ripy, Jr. who then held the position of master distiller. In 1981 when the French conglomerate Pernod Ricard acquired the business, the distillery was renamed again. This time it was called Boulevard Distillery. December 21, 2001, the distillery received the name it deserves: Wild Turkey Distillery. Halfway 2009 the Feathered Beastie was acquired by the Campari Group, originating from Gaspare Campari who started to make his signature drink in the 1860s. The Turkey started its life as an American, then became French and now can boast of being Italian-American. The bourbon is still as straight and robust as ever, although it gained the name Wild Turkey only in 1942. There is a story attached to that as well.

Possibly to honor the original founder of the distillery, J.P. Ripy launched the brands Sam Stephens and J.W. Stephens in 1888, alongside his namesake brand J.P. Ripy whiskey. He also delivered barrels to distributors and merchants who sold the whiskey, more often than not blended with other whiskeys, under their own brand names. Around 1905 the brand names Ripy Bros and Old Hardie were introduced. Up to 1918 more brand names were launched, but they didn't survive or were sold to other distilleries after Repeal. This was a common practice in those days. T.B. Ripy must have been a remarkable man with good commercial instincts.

Gary and Mardee Regan wrote in their *Book of Bourbon* (1995) that T.B. developed plans at the end of the 19th century to ship whiskey to Germany. After maturation it would be shipped back to the US again to be bottled, somehow as a tax-advantage. When asked about the story, Jimmy Russell, the current Master Distiller, had to laugh, "We have to pay taxes when it is distilled. Right away. Not like the Scots who have to pay taxes after bottling. I don't know who told that story, but it is not true."

To clarify Jimmy's quote: the proof gallons distilled are recorded and tracked through to barreling. The distilleries pay an Advalorem Tax – like a property tax – throughout the maturation process. Other taxes are paid at bottling, primarily the Federal Excise Tax which is the most costly of all taxes.

In 1935, two years after the ending of Prohibition, T.B.'s sons continued the brand name Ripy Bros and entered into a distribution contract with Austin Nichols, whose general manager Tom McCarthy was a big fan of the Ripy whiskey. In 1942 he invited three bridge-friends on their yearly turkey hunt and took a couple of bottles of his favorite tipple with him. The men liked the whiskey so much that it acquired the name Wild Turkey whiskey, commemorating the annual hunt. In that same year McCarthy registered the brand name. So, when Austin Nichols acquired the distillery in 1972 from Gould, the former had already owned the brand name for 30 odd years. Remarkably, the brand name Wild Turkey is 60 years older than the eponymous distillery.

For Jimmy Russell it is all Turkey Business, regardless of the history. He has been with the distillery for over half a century and shows a mixture of love and pride when walking on the grounds. According to Jimmy, "Most people leave here early. They start working at the distillery at 7:00 in the morning and leave around 3:30 in the afternoon. They have little farms to tend to. It's been like that since the 19th century." Jimmy's son Ed also works for Wild Turkey and has been around for more than 25 years. He is one of five tasters who select the barrels before bottling.

Wild Turkey produces two types of whiskey: a straight bourbon and a straight rye. Fermentation takes up to 72 hours at 32 degrees Celsius. Only one yeast strain is used, which is kept alive in a big vessel, fed with rye and malted barley. The fermented mash is distilled first in a beer still,

129

then in a doubler, which results in a liquid containing 60% ABV. Before being poured into barrels, it is diluted to 55% ABV. The warehouses are partially on the same premises as the distillery, partly around Lawrenceburg and across from the Four Roses Distillery, the oldest one dating back to the 1890s. The barrels are stacked six or seven high. A warehouse usually contains around 20,000 barrels with aging whiskey. Different ages are spread around the warehouses, to minimize risks. The original 19th century wooden stillhouse is intact, but due to health and safety regulations the stills were relocated to a new stillhouse made of iron and steel. The barrels are bought from Independent Staves Co. cooperage. Not all used barrels are sold to the Scottish whisky industry, which is the common practice. A small portion was sold to China, where they were used for wooden floors. According to Jimmy Russell those floors are as good and strong as the whiskey with which the planks are impregnated. Barrels selected for bottling are transported to a bottling facility in Arkansas. On the cozy visitor center veranda, Jimmy recalled the anecdote about T.B. Ripy and his German plans. "We do sell barrels of Wild Turkey to Germany. They bottle it themselves, under private label." It seems nothing has changed in that respect, compared with the 19th century.

The annual production is slightly more than 1 million liters. Wild Turkey Straight Bourbon is bottled at 80 and 101 proofs, respectively 40 and 50.5% ABV. It is a spicy whiskey with a bite. Wild Turkey Rare Breed is a small batch version and Kentucky Spirit an 8-9 years old single barrel expression. Both are bottled at cask strength. Jimmy's namesake Russell's Reserve is a 10-year-old small batch bourbon, 90 proof (45% ABV). Wild Turkey Straight Rye is bottled at 101 proof, at 5-6 years old.

In the current American whiskey industry there are not many people around like Jimmy Russell. He could truly be called a living monument. Since he has been working at the distillery from 1954, he can state that he has worked with the last Ripy connected to the Turkey Business. Jimmy learned how to distill from Bill Hughes, same name as Jack Daniel's master distiller in 1887, but not a relative. It shows how confusing the history of American whiskey can be. In 1954 Kentucky had 48 independent distilleries, compared with fewer than 10 today. Despite the frequent takeovers and mergers, Jimmy keeps track and is a walking whiskey encyclopedia. He also is one of the judges at the annual International Wines & Spirits Competition. When asked if he enjoys wine and single malts as well, he smiles and answers, "No, for me, it's bourbon, or iced-tea."

***

Wild Turkey Distillery had many names in the past and the bourbon still has various nicknames: The Dirty Bird, Gobble Gobble, Thunder Chicken, Boat Gas, Kickin' Chicken.

The same can be said of blues legend John Lee Hooker, who had the habit of record label hopping, common practice among blues musicians. Hooker's records can therefore be found under various labels. To avoid legal action he recorded under many different names: John Lee Booker, John Lee Cooker, Texas Slim, The Boogie Man, Little Pork Chops, Birmingham Sam, Johnny Williams and Delta John. Unfortunately some dishonest record company owners credited themselves with original compositions, paying musicians a flat fee and basically robbing them of future royalties.

Hooker's output was phenomenal, with more than 100 albums to his credit, recorded between 1948 and 2001, the year he died. Between 2001 and 2010 at least 16 new compilations were released by various record companies. It is a testament to his enduring popularity.

Nothing of that kind could have been predicted from his early childhood. Born in a sharecropper's family in 1917, in the area around Clarksdale, Mississippi, the youngest of eleven siblings, John Lee was first exposed to religious music, his father being a part-time preacher. When he was four years old his father took off and within the year his mother remarried a blues singer. It was this William Moore who introduced the young John Lee to the guitar and influenced his unique form of playing, a fact Hooker would mention time and again as an adult. His style is totally different from the Delta Blues that developed in the same era and it's been his trademark ever since. He didn't care much for sticking to meter and made up his own songs on the spot, accompanying himself with a piano boogie-like sound. His heavy foot tapping was an integral part of his performance.

Hooker didn't stay in the Delta long, running away at age 15, never to return to his parental home. At first he tried to make a living as a musician in Memphis, Tennessee, playing at Beale Street and juggling the odd job to make ends meet. After several moves he settled in Detroit, Michigan, in 1948, where he worked at the Ford Motor Company. At the time there were mostly pianists in town and when Hooker entered the East Side blues bars he was soon picked up and became popular, especially when he switched to electric guitar. That same year he made his first recording, the seminal "Boogie Chillun" that turned into a great hit. It was also the first time that a song was stolen from him. In this particular case by Bernie Besman, who unashamedly credited himself as co-composer. Since Hooker was illiterate, Besman had the nerve to claim that John Lee didn't write his own compositions. This was extremely unfair, since Hooker was a great improv artist who could make lyrical poetry on the spot during a recording or a live performance.

In the early 1970s this finally backfired on Besman when ZZ Top covered "Boogie Chillun," naming it La Grange instead. A dispute over copyrights arose and unwittingly John Lee Hooker's first recorded song became the cause of new legislation. When a local court eventually decided the song was in the public domain and hence no earlier copyrights could be claimed, the U.S. Supreme Court refused to overrule the decision. It aroused anger in the music industry and many major players effectively lobbied against the ruling. This resulted in a Congressional Bill many years later, which was signed into law by then-President Bill Clinton. Sadly Hooker didn't benefit from it, since he had long lost the rights to his early recordings.

The Bihari Brothers were of the same breed as Besman and not ashamed of claiming a Hooker song written or co-written by themselves or their aliases Taub and Josea, thus ensuring they received the royalties. To their credit it must be said that they gave a broad audience to many artists who would otherwise have been largely unnoticed. On the surface, however, such practices certainly look like taking someone else's intellectual property. John Lee Hooker continued to record songs with an astounding number of record companies: Ace, Atco, Atlantic, Bluesway, Chess, Crown, Impulse!, King, Modern, Point Blank, Polydor, Savoy, Specialty, Vee-Jay, and Verve.

In the 1950s Hooker showed up in Chicago regularly, where he would be seen playing at Maxwell Market, sometimes with the likes of Muddy Waters and B.B. King, the latter also having started his musical career in Memphis. Since Hooker made up most of his songs on the spot, not caring too much for a steady rhythm or a specific duration of a song, it wasn't easy for most musicians to accompany him. He could easily turn a simple riff into a 15-minute poem, repeating it in his unique, immediately recognizable style of playing, foot tapping and distinctive singing. Due to the rise of rock 'n' roll the traditional blues took a backseat and for some years Hooker and many of his fellow musicians who stayed true to the blues experienced a serious decline in bookings.

This would change with the 1960s blues revival when many white blues musicians came to the fore, both in the UK and in the USA. This culminated for John Lee Hooker in one of the monumental blues albums of the early 1970s. He teamed up with a talented young American blues-rock group Canned Heat. The name was derived from a Tommy Johnson song in which the old Delta blues man referred to an alcoholic beverage drunk during Prohibition. The record *Hooker 'n' Heat* was an instant success and probably for the first time in his career Hooker experienced substantial earnings from a recording.

Hooker made an excellent comeback, continuing to perform and record. Later he preferred to be accompanied by larger groups of musicians, while concentrating on his singing. By the end of the 1970s the general interest in blues waned and Hooker disappeared into the background. But in 1989, he celebrated a huge second comeback when the award winning CD *The Healer* became incredibly successful. Hooker is accompanied successively by Carlos Santana, Bonnie Raitt, Los Lobos, Robert Cray, George Thorogood, Charlie Musselwhite and Canned Heat, but Hooker is right there, on every track. As a direct consequence he started touring again and ended up opening a nightclub in San Francisco, naming it after one of his greatest hits, the John Lee Hooker's Boom Boom Room. The next few years he managed to stay on the road until he rather suddenly fell seriously ill. A planned overseas tour had to be cancelled and Europe would never again see the Boogie Man. He died in Los Altos, California on June 21, 2001, age 83.

John Lee Hooker is a rare breed in the world of the blues. His mesmerizing style of blues playing and his stream of consciousness lyrics are unique and inimitable. His music sometimes evokes an atmosphere like Jack Kerouac's *On The Road*. Hooker's voice, seemingly a bit harsh at first but developing a multi-layered character when listened to intensively, reminds me of Wild Turkey, and especially the Rare Breed expression, that barrel-proof bottling. Hooker was barrel proof too, as can be heard in his famous song "One Bourbon, One Scotch, One Beer." Let's hail once more, a cheer for bourbon and blues! If that doesn't get you In the Mood, his duet with Bonnie Raitt will!

Jimmy Russell, Master Distiller Wild Turkey.

A Barrel Full of Blues
The Blue Grass Coopers and Muddy Waters

A cask - or barrel - as Americans prefer, can add 60-70% of the flavor to the eventual whisky it will render. Having such a tremendous influence on the drink, it deserves some scrutiny. The Speyside Cooperage, located just outside the tiny village of Craigellachie, in the heart of the Scottish Speyside, offers not only a very interesting tour but also a beautiful visitor's center and shop with refreshments. Until recently it was the only independent cooperage in Scottish hands. The brothers Douglas and William Taylor sold their company to François Frères Tonnellerie, an old and respected family-owned French firm that has been manufacturing oak casks for the wine industry for over a century. Only 5% of the annual production from the Speyside Cooperage consists of entirely new casks. The rest will be repaired, rejuvenated, enlarged or recycled.

Most whisky casks in Scotland begin their lives as whiskey barrels made in cooperages located in the USA. The largest is the Bluegrass Cooperage in Louisville, KY, founded in 1945. They exclusively produce barrels from American white oak (*Quercus alba*). The annual output is around 500,000 barrels a year.

Some time ago my wife and I visited the Bluegrass Cooperage for an interview with the manager and an extensive photo-shoot. Thanks to our friends at Jack Daniel's everything was well-prepared for our visit. Someone from

HQ was even summoned to be present. Only later we understood that is standard policy at Brown-Forman (B-F). They want to know who visits, what is said and what is presented. No dropping in casually here!

After an extensive explanation about sustainability and forestry, operations plant manager Neil McElroy personally took us on a tour of the various departments. First we viewed the delivery platform. Here product is delivered daily from which the eventual parts of the barrel will be assembled. The planks are sawn before transport and primarily come from Jackson, Ohio, Albany, New York and Clifton, Tennessee. The sawing factories in these states mainly buy the felled trees from loggers. The trees will be air-dried for six months and then further dried in a kiln. When the degree of humidity in the wood is lowered to 12%, the first sawing phase starts. The bark is taken from the wood and the tree is sawn in half. The two halves – lengthwise – are sawn in half again. The four remaining long pieces render planks of 38 inches each. Cutting the tree in this way takes the radials in the wood into optimal account and prevents the eventual barrel from leaking. The planks are delivered to the Bluegrass Cooperage where they will be shaped into heads, ends and staves.

The Iron Department produces hoops from a long section of flexible iron band. A special knife cuts the pieces to the desired length and another mechanical device drills two holes on either side, after which the ends are fastened together. The fastener nails carry an identifier, the letter B - for Bluegrass or Brown-Forman, whatever you prefer.

At the Heading Department the ends of the barrel are manufactured. Pieces of planks are sawn at the specified length, shaven and punctured. The resulting holes will later hold wooden pegs. At first the ends are square and have to be rounded by a special shaving and sawing machine. Then the round ends are led through an oven wherein they are lightly toasted. After cooling down, the edges of the ends are greased with bees wax.

At the Stave Department more planks are sawn to a precise length and fine-shaven to get as smooth a surface as possible. The ready-to-use staves are then transported on a small cart to the barrel raisers, who place the staves in an iron base ring. Normally a barrel contains between 29 and 31 staves. An experienced barrel raiser can raise about 270 barrels in an eight-hour shift. When all staves are placed in the ring, another temporary iron ring is shifted over the top end of the barrel.

A belt takes the barrel-to-be through a steam tunnel wherein the oak wood is somewhat "softened." This prevents breaking of the staves when they are forced into the hoops at the Buffalo Department, also known as The House of Pain. When the barrels come out of the steam tunnel a winch presses the staves together and the barrel raiser throws another hoop around the barrel. Then the flames do their work. First the inside of the barrel is toasted. This process ensures that the flavor and color components of the wood come to the surface. After toasting, the barrels are transported to the Buffalo Machine that tightens them in order to secure another pair of hoops. Again the barrels have to face the fire. They are conveyed into an oven and their interiors exposed to a burning fire for about 35 seconds. This charring brings even more flavor components to the fore but also serves as a filter for the whiskey that will eventually be put in the barrel. There are four grades of charring, named grade 1, 2, 3 and alligator. The latter is the heaviest char and the name refers to the surface of the blackened wood, which somewhat resembles the hide of the reptile.

When the charring is completed the barrel is moved to the Finishing Department. The head-up machine places the top and bottom ends after which the barrel has to cool down. The temporary hoops are taken off and replaced by the definitive hoops, usually six in total. Then the cooper picks one of the broadest staves to bore the bunghole. Approximately one liter of water is poured into the barrel, which will then be pressurized and closed with a rubber stop. This is done to check for possible leaks. At the end station every single cask is re-checked and eventual leaks are repaired. Now the barrel is ready and waiting in the warehouse to be transported by a truck to the customer- a distillery.

The Bluegrass Cooperage is owned by B-F, so the majority of the production is destined for its flagship Jack Daniel. Each day seven truckloads leave Louisville, Kentucky, heading for Lynchburg, Tennessee. A big contrast with B-F's small boutique distillery Woodford Reserve, which receives about 110 barrels every other week. Eventually 95% of all these barrels will end up in Scotland. Old Forester, made in Louisville, Kentucky, is also part of the B-F family and therefore receives its barrels from Bluegrass.

The joint cooperages in the USA are said to only use 0.1% of the global hardwood reserve yearly. B-F, the cooperage and the University of Tennessee cooperate directly in a program to cut trees and replant new seedlings responsibly. It takes 70 to 80 years before a white oak tree is suitable for barrel making. The trees mainly come from privately owned forests in southern Minnesota, Missouri, Indiana, Arkansas, Tennessee, Kentucky, Ohio and West Virginia. Cutting trees is a continuous process, 12 months a year. The cutting is done selectively, for example in areas that need thinning to allow for new growth.

The wood alone takes up 60-70% of the total cost of making a barrel. Only 50% of the delivered planks will continue their life as a barrel - the rest is pulped and serves as fuel for the kilns at the sawmills. For a while some of the wood not used for production was shipped to China, where it was made into flooring. A nice example of zero waste management.

Today around 230 people work at the Bluegrass Cooperage. The labor is heavy, but there are few personnel changes. If an apprentice survives the first two years, he usually sticks around. There are four levels of experience – grade four up to grade one. During our visit we met the only female cooper in Kentucky, Melissa Kappel. After more than four years of service she had reached grade one and receives the highest salary a cooper can earn. The coopers are members of the United Auto Workers Union, who negotiates the salaries with their employer. In Scotland that is totally different, since the Scottish coopers are being paid by the cask.

American law dictates that bourbon can only mature in new American oak barrels. This law was introduced to stimulate forestry and surrounding industries in the USA. The Scots profit from that regulation, since the surplus of used barrels has to go somewhere. A second-hand barrel currently costs approximately 80 dollars, but prices may vary regarding supply and demand. Barrels are shipped to Scotland disassembled, in staves. Having arrived at its new habitat, usually the Speyside Cooperage in Craigellachie, the barrel is reassembled and enlarged from 200 to 250 liters. From now on it is referred to as a cask or a hogshead. Some distilleries, like the famed Springbank in Campbeltown on the Kintyre Peninsula, maintain their own cooperage but rely on a steady stream of ex-bourbon barrels imported from the USA.

When visiting the Speyside Cooperage one can see familiar names, casks with Maker's Mark, Jack Daniel's, Jim Beam or Buffalo Trace stamped on the head. Maybe two decades ago they were part of a sturdy oak tree in the USA. Now a Scottish hogshead waiting for repair or rejuvenation and transport to a Scottish distillery, to be filled with new-make single malt whisky.

After four to eight years of service in the bourbon industry, the barrel-transformed-into-a-cask will be used up to three more times in Scotland, typically for 10 to 12 year periods. After that it is exhausted and the remaining wood

143

is put to use as barbecue fuel or garden furniture. From acorn to retired cask is a lifespan of 120 years.

***

Coopering is a profession dominated by men. The work is physically demanding. The original material has to be bent and shaped into a form that will serve a distinct purpose: to store the colorless liquid that will mature into an amber treasure over the years. The cooper is sturdy and persevering, proudly strong.

He brings to mind that proud blues singer and guitarist who bent his raw material into muscular blue notes and sang powerful lyrics, inspiring many bluesicians for decades to come – McKinley Morganfield, better known as Muddy Waters. Like so many blues men he came from the Delta, that specific area around the place where the Yazoo and Mississippi Rivers meet, which spawned such richness in musical talent. However he would become predominantly know as the Father of the Chicago Blues.

His birth is a bit of a myth, since various documents show differing birth years, from 1913 to 1915. Waters himself, superstitious to the core and feeding the myth, would relate in songs that he was born in the seventh hour of the seventh day of the seventh month, a gypsy having predicted his coming to this world. A fact is that his mother died when he was very young and he was raised by his grandmother. She might have been the one responsible for giving him his nickname Muddy, because he enjoyed playing in the mud as a toddler. The nickname stuck to the boy, and as an adult, he changed his name officially to Muddy Waters. Around the age of thirteen he worked as a field hand and took up the harmonica to teach himself the basics of the blues. Under the influence of Son House's and Robert Johnson's playing, Muddy took on the guitar and learned to play. At first he imitated the two great Delta men at local gigs, but slowly developed his own powerful style with microtones and a strong voice. In the latter echoes can be heard of Son House's singing and in Muddy's guitar technique Robert Johnson's notes resound.

Muddy Waters boasted about his virility in many of his songs and performances. Apparently this side of his personality started in his earlier years in the Delta. When he left for Chicago in 1940, there were already two ex-Mrs. Morganfields and a child with a girlfriend who was married to someone else. For a couple of years Muddy played in clubs and exploited a juke joint, since the music didn't bring him enough money. He went back to Mississippi for a while, working at Stovall Plantation where he grew up. This is where blues researcher and writer Alan Lomax found him and recorded Muddy for the first time ever. However, those recordings would not appear on a record for a long, long time.

In 1943 Muddy definitively established himself in Chicago, helped by Big Bill Broonzy, who already played the circuit and offered him the evening opening slot. That mustn't have been a thankful job since he had to play over the crowd with an acoustic guitar. Things went easier two

years later when he was given an electric guitar by his
uncle. He became better known in the years to come and
finally broke through in 1948 with "I Can't Be Satisfied,"
an obvious reference to his zest for women and a boast
about his manhood. The song would become the platform
on which Muddy built his name as the King of the Electric
Chicago Blues and influenced many guitarists, rock and
blues bands to come. More "virile" songs followed, many
of them composed by bass player Willie Dixon who played
in one of Waters' early bands, along with Otis Spann, Little
Walter and Jimmy Rogers, all becoming stars in their own
right. "I Am Ready," "Hoochie Coochie Man" and "I Just
Want to Make Love" hit the charts, emphasizing the macho image that was now firmly Muddy's trademark. Off the
stage he was as creative as on the stage, remarrying and
fathering more children, some of whom would only later
in life be introduced to their biological father.

In the song "Gypsy Woman" Muddy refers to the origins of his sexual prowess. Another major hit from that
period became his musical signature and would be ad-
opted in the 1960s by a young English rock band as their
name. The tune was called "Rollin' Stone." Said band also
derived one of their first hits from Muddy's first one,
when they released "I Can't Get No. . . .Satisfaction." At
the turn of the 1960s Led Zeppelin loosely based their
worldwide hit "Whole Lotta Love" on another Muddy song,
"You Need Love." These are just two examples of how influential Muddy Waters became over the years. That didn't
happen overnight. Firstly the Hoochie Coochie Man had

to firmly establish himself in the Chicago blues scene. His great competitor in the early 1950s was Howlin' Wolf, with whom he regularly swapped musicians for his band such as Hubert Sumlin, an excellent guitarist.

Muddy's antagonist, shortly referred to as "The Wolf", was known to be a show man who would use tricks to embellish his performances, for instance by climbing in the curtains on stage and slowly lowering himself again, continuing to sing the entire time. Like Waters he enjoyed presenting himself as a real macho and one of his acts was comprised of him putting an open bottle of coke in his trousers, with the opening peeping out, putting his thumb on the bottle opening, shaking it vigorously and squirting the drink over the first rows of people in the audience. Howlin' Wolf was a tyrant, demanding and even humiliating his band members on stage. One time Hubert Sumlin had enough of it and walked offstage, leaving to play with Muddy Waters for a while, but returning after things had settled down between him and Wolf.

As an interesting sideline, Frank Zappa reckoned Wolf to be one of his great inspirations and that might have been a source of some of the outrageous performances and sexually explicit lyrics FZ and the Mothers, most notably when Flo and Eddie joined the group, presented to the public in the 1960s and 1970s. Zappa was also a tyrant to his band members, demanding the highest quality from them while performing. Many of FZ's songs are rooted in the blues and doo-wop, and occasionally he played a mean blues solo himself, as can be heard for instance in "Merely a Blues in A" on *Zappa Plays Zappa*. Anyway, Muddy, Howlin' Wolf and FZ had more than music in common.

Muddy's band became a hotbed of blues talents and he continued to add new members to his line up, among whom harmonica players James Cotton, Big Walter Horton and Jerry Portnoy. In 1958 Muddy appeared in England for the first time and blew the audience away with his powerful electric blues. Back in the USA he recorded his first live album at the 1960 New Port Jazz Festival. Crowds in both countries who had been accustomed to acoustic country blues took an immediate liking to the "new" raw, electrified blues that made Muddy the undisputed King of the Electric Blues. He returned to England in the early 1970s, playing along with various guitarists like the Irish guitar magician Rory Gallagher, Steve Winwood and Eric Clapton, the latter covering various Waters-songs with his super group Cream.

In 1973 Muddy suffered a severe setback when his wife of many years, Geneva, died of cancer. He quit smoking, settled in a Chicago suburb and took a step back from the scene. In the mean time, more illegitimate children showed up on his doorstep. When persuaded to perform at a concert in Florida, Muddy met a 19-year-old girl named Marva Jean Brooks, who became the next Mrs. Waters, although Muddy usually referred to her as Sunshine.

His 1976 rendition of "Mannish Boy" must have inspired him to get back to work since it was launched on a record and used for a soundtrack in The Band's swansong *The Last Waltz*. Again a new and talented blues harp man appeared by Muddy's side. His name was Paul Butterfield.

No one less than Johnny Winter caused a sort of come-back for Muddy Waters when he produced the album *Hard Again*, on which the fabulous albino guitarist played along-side Waters, James Cotton, Pinetop Perkins, Jerry Portnoy, Luther Johnson, Calvin Jones and Willy Smith. It is con-sidered by many the best Waters band ever. The coopera-tion between Waters and Winter was very fruitful. Not only did *Hard Again* earn a Grammy, but a successful tour also followed and three more albums were released over the years, each doing extremely well. In 1981 both men per-formed for the last time together at Chicago Fest and en-thused a new young crowd to the blues, Muddy's Chicago Blues! One of his last performances was with Eric Clapton when the latter did a show in Florida, late 1982.

The Father of the Electric Chicago Blues' health rapidly deteriorated over that same winter and on April 30, 1983 his mojo finally stopped working. At age 68 he left a legacy that transcends the blues realm. During his life he not only "invented" the Chicago Blues, but influenced many musical styles, be it future blues, jazz, folk, country, R&B or rock' n' roll. This man, who was instrumental in getting Chuck Berry to sign his first recording contract, could have no better epitaph than the title of one of his own songs: "The Blues Had a Baby and They Named It Rock 'n' Roll."

Muddy Waters' Chicago blues, rooted in the Delta, traveled to England and was put to a different use, like the American barrels being re-shaped and re-used by the Scot-tish distillers decades later. Chicago blues returned to the

USA via the likes of Eric Clapton, just as the Scottish single malts now crowd the walls of many American bars.

There are many bourbons you can savor when listening to Muddy Waters. Basically you can't be satisfied with one in particular. However, if I had to choose the proverbial "only one on an desert island," this is the bourbon to have, especially made by Heaven Hill for another great music legend, Willie Nelson.

It's called Old Whiskey River, after one of his favorite songs. It comes complete with Willie's bandana and an autographed guitar pick.

The Bluegrass Cooperage, Louisville, Kentucky.

Master Charge
Rip van Winkle and Albert Collins

One of the famous names in the history of bourbon is Julian P. Van Winkle, Sr., also know as "Pappy," a nickname he earned while a young whiskey salesman. His credo was, "We make fine bourbon at a profit if we can, at a loss if we must, but always fine bourbon."

Today the Van Winkle bourbons are made by Buffalo Trace distillery, but that was not always the case. Pappy started in the late 1800s as a traveling salesman working for the W.L. Weller & Son Distillery. At the time it was not strictly a distillery but more of a wholesaler and blender of various liquors. Pappy became infatuated with quality and wanted to make the best bourbon available. He teamed up with financial wizard Alex Farnsley and together they managed to purchase W.L. Weller and eventually merged with the A.Ph. Stitzel Distillery, which actually manufactured the whiskey for Weller. Now the men had full control of the entire production and sales chain. After the successful merger the company was known as the Stitzel-Weller Distillery. Pappy began to create famous brands, the thing for which he was born: W.L. Weller, Old Fitzgerald, Rebel Yell and Cabin Still.

The recipes were somewhat different from your usual bourbon, not containing a proportion of rye in the mash bill to balance the corn, but wheat instead. Maker's Mark does the same today. Somehow Farnsley and Van Winkle

managed to survive Prohibition and in 1935 Pappy opened
a brand new Stitzel-Weller Distillery in the southern part
of Louisville, Kentucky. His son-in-law King McClure joined
the management team shortly after World War II. McClure
had been able to get his hands on corn during the war to
sustain the continuation of whiskey production, which was
quite an achievement in itself, considering the demand for
food. About the same time, Pappy's son Julian, Jr. joined
and in 1947 Stitzel-Weller was reigned by what was called
The Triumvirate, aka "The Father, Son and Holy Ghost."
It proved to be a fantastic team until Pappy died in 1965
at the age of 91, semi-retired. He had never been able to
completely leave the business. The whiskey industry lost
not only a fine craftsman but also a great entertainer who
made a lasting impression on whoever met him.

As happens so often when the patriarch of the family dies, the siblings fell out. Julian, Jr.'s sister, nicknamed
"Rip," wanted to sell the business. Under great pressure
from Rip, her husband King, and a cunning corporate lawyer, Julian, Jr. finally gave in to selling the company to a
large competitor who would ultimately merge into Diageo
many years later. This was exactly the outcome Julian, Jr.
was trying to avoid.

The origin of Julian's sister's nickname leaves some
room for speculation. It certainly did not mean "Rest in
Peace" since Pappy would have fiercely opposed selling out
a small family company that made excellent bourbon to a
large one that was mainly interested in producing cheap
bulk whiskey. The nickname might have come instead

from a Washington Irving character of the *Knickerbocker Tales*: Rip van Winkle, an idle, hen-pecked man of Dutch descent living in the Catskill Mountains of New York. The story goes that he escaped his wife one day to go hunting in the woods, there encountering a group of bearded men dressed in old-fashioned Dutch clothing who were bowling on the grass. He drank some of their liquor, which tasted to him like "Hollands," a form of jenever or gin that is still made in the Netherlands. Upon drinking several glasses, he fell asleep for 20 years. When he awoke and returned to his village, he had missed, among other things, the American Revolution.

Julian, Jr. did however keep the brand name Van Winkle and some old stock with which he could continue to make bourbon of the quality for which Pappy had always fought. He no longer distilled, instead concentrating on blending, bottling and selling first-rate bourbon. Soon his son Julian III became part of the business. Sadly Julian, Jr. died of cancer in 1981, only 67 years old. By then he had established Van Winkle as a brand famous for its old bourbons, leaving the memory of Pappy intact. In fact Pappy Van Winkle's Family Reserve 20-year-old was the oldest bottled bourbon available for quite some time. Irving's story fuels the imagination and gives room for thought about the Pappy van Winkle Family Reserve that had lain dormant for 20 years before being bottled as an outstanding bourbon.

Due to the existing stocks Julian III could continue to produce beautiful old bourbons. He managed to buy the old Hoffman Distillery, located on the banks of the Salt River in Lawrenceburg, Kentucky in 1983, where he stored and bottled his bourbon from then on. In 1998 the 20-year-old Pappy Van Winkle Family Reserve won the highest score ever in the World Spirits Championship, a 99, immediately followed by its younger sibling, the 15-year-old Old Rip Van Winkle. In 2001 he welcomed his own son Preston into the company, thus involving the fourth generation of Van Winkles. That same year Julian III entered into a joint venture with Buffalo Trace Distillery, formerly known as Ancient Age Distillery. He wanted to have access to younger whiskey and diversify, in order to survive. Since then Buffalo Trace has distilled all "new" Van Winkle bourbons according to the old recipe that originated from the Stitzel-Weller Distillery. The range has been broadened with a Van Winkle Kentucky Straight Rye whiskey, 13 years of age. Thus the heritage from Pappy who insisted on using wheat instead of rye to complement the corn is not 100% intact. Rebel Yell, Old Fitzgerald, Cabin Still and W.L. Weller continue to be produced, but other companies own the brands (Heaven Hill and Buffalo Trace). The Stitzel-Weller Distillery permanently closed its doors in 1992, although the warehouses are still in use.

The Van Winkle bottlings are high in demand, they are rare and Julian van Winkle III is truly a master blender, following in the footsteps of his father and grandfather.

***

When sippin' that master's blend I like to listen to the master of the Telecaster: Albert Collins, aka The Texas Razor Blade and the Iceman. Like Pappy van Winkle he was a great entertainer and one you wouldn't forget once you had seen him perform. He seamlessly blended Texas, Mississippi and Chicago Blues like the Van Winkles have done with their highly praised bourbons. Pappy Van Winkle was a stickler for detail and quality, something Collins insisted on as well. He favored an open tuning on his guitar, used his thumb instead of a pick and insisted on playing a specific Fender Telecaster. These idiosyncrasies were not unlike Pappy's demand for wheat instead of rye in the mash bill.

Albert Collins was born and raised in Texas and is said to have been a cousin of Lightnin' Hopkins. At the age of 20 he formed his first bands and played the clubs in Houston. Six years later, in 1958, he made his first recordings and scored a best seller with the instrumental single "Frosty" a few years later. During the recording a very young Janis Joplin and Johnny Winter were in the audience. The former predicted the million selling success of the single, according to Collins.

Unlike many other blues musicians, he moved to Kansas City, Missouri instead of Chicago. That was in 1965 and the days of the big Kansas City music scene were already over. The city that could boast the birth of Count Basie's Barons of Rhythm had lost its famous son a decade before when John Hammond had lured Basie to New York. Collins played and became famous, even got married, but couldn't find a decent recording studio in his new hometown. In 1968 Bob "The Bear" Hite of Canned Heat came over to hear him play at a concert in Texas and convinced Collins to move to Los Angeles, which he did. Hite was instrumental in having him record his first album *Love Can Be Found Anywhere*, which was released by Imperial Records in 1969. The Texas Razorblade became the hero of the Cool Blues on the West coast and regularly performed in the Fillmore West in San Francisco. Not too proud for any job, he delighted in driving his band's tour bus. In 1978 came his great international break when he signed up with Alligator Records to cut the award winning *Ice Pickin'* album. The highly talented Texas Razorblade had been playing in relative obscurity to the rest of the world. After the groundbreaking *Ice Pickin'* he spearheaded a worldwide revival of the electric blues in the 1980s.

With his backing band The Ice Breakers, Collins now toured throughout the USA, in Europe and even Japan. In the Alligator years the Iceman was encouraged to sing more and as a result wrote his famous "Master Charge" and "Conversation with Collins," assisted by his Kansas wife Gwendolyn - proving his spouse was also creatively fruitful. So was his marriage with the reptile logo-ed company. It lasted for more than a decade during which seven albums were recorded and launched, among which *Frostbite!* and *Live in Japan*. Johnny Copeland, with whom Albert Collins grew up in Houston, cut a record with him and a much younger Robert Cray, who had heard Collins play when still in high school, then deciding to venture on his own career as a blues guitarist. The resulting *Showdown!* won three Grammies, one for each guitarist.

The audience loved his entertaining style of playing. One of his favorite tricks was to use a power cord over a few hundred meters long. Collins would step off the stage, continuing to play whilst walking through the audience and even outside on the pavement. Personally I have fond memories of seeing him do this when he performed at North Sea Jazz in 1983, in The Hague, government city of my home country The Netherlands. In the film documentary *Antones: Austin's Home of the Blues* Collins even walks further, into a restaurant, and orders a pizza, continues to play and returns to the stage, having a pizza man deliver his order 10 minutes later. He also made an appearance in the movie *Adventures in Babysitting* where he forces the children to improvise a song, before they may escape, stating "nobody leaves this place without singin' the blues."

Collin's lyrics are wickedly funny as in "Master Charge," where he finds his lady spending far too much on his credit card. In "Conversation with Collins," a woman returns home from a night out with girlfriends far after curfew, having left her man to babysit for "a few hours." The guitar speaks, literally "playing" a dialogue starting with the woman telling the man "sorry, baby," the man responding to the woman she is a "dirty motherf@?8!!" On the song "Snowed in" from *Frostbite!* Collins struggles with his truck, trying to start the engine in the bitter cold. Since he wrote most of these songs with his wife Gwen, the couple must have shared a great sense of humor.

In the late 1980s Collins moved to Las Vegas, Nevada and signed with Point Blank, part of Virgin Records. He continued to gather fame in the years to come, with performances in Spain, England and Switzerland. In the last country he became ill after a show in July 1993 and was taken into hospital where he was diagnosed with cancer of the lungs and the liver. He left Switzerland with the message that he had possibly only four months to live. It proved to be a sad truth. The Iceman died on November 24 that same year and was buried at the Davis Memorial Park in Las Vegas, Nevada.

Albert Collins will be remembered by many, since he not only influenced a whole school of guitarists but also worked with many of them, among whom Stevie Ray Vaughan who considered him a great influence on his own playing, B.B. King, Eric Clapton, Jimmy Page and Keith Richards. His style of playing is inimitable and immediately recognizable, as his many song titles. He had a preference for cool titles: "Ice Pickin'", "Cold, Cold Feeling," "Snowed In," "Ice Pick," "Avalanche," "Frosty," "Don't Lose Your Cool," "Cold Snap." The list seems endless. His first single ever, which he recorded for Kangaroo, back in his Texan days, was called "The Freeze." That must have been the kick-start for The Iceman.

I am not a proponent of ice in my whiskey. It tends to anesthetize the palate, so I suggest sippin' some neat Van Winkles with some undiluted Collins blues. Two first class products from two American master crafters!

159

Pappy Van Winkle's Family Reserve, labeled by hand.

Van Winkle closely cooperates with Buffalo Trace.

Tavern Tales
Oscar Getz and Sugar Blue

Bardstown, Kentucky, is considered America's bourbon capital, much like the cozy Dufftown, Speyside, Scotland is for single malts. That's where the comparison stops immediately. Where Dufftown is crowned with a 300-year-old belfry on the central square and crossroads, the center of Bardstown hosts a courthouse that is 200 years younger. However on the southwest corner of the square a building proudly stands that dates back to the 1770s: Old Talbott Tavern.

The United States of America signed the Declaration of Independence on July 4, 1776. It was the official start of the Revolutionary War against the British. It would last for five years and with the assistance of the French, the USA eventually won. The British surrendered on October 17, 1781. In that year Talbott Tavern was already in existence for two years, albeit not under that particular name. One can safely assume that the tavern hosted soldiers from both sides. In pioneer days places like the Talbott Tavern offered travelers a place to stay and also served as resting places for the stagecoaches. In the second half of the 18th century this was the western end of the stagecoach services that ran from Pennsylvania and Virginia. On offer were drinks and food, in addition to a place to stay for the night. The thick brick walls not only saw soldiers come and go, but a whole range of famous and notorious people.

On October 17, 1779 the French king-in-exile Louis Philippe arrived at the tavern with his two brothers and a large group of servants and courtiers. When the building was renovated in 1927, murals were found that were supposedly painted by the king's servants. John Fitch, the inventor of the steamboat, was one of the regular guests around 1800. He is buried at the cemetery in Bardstown. In 1822 Abraham Lincoln, then a 13-year-old boy, stayed at the tavern with his parents, who were involved in a court case over land ownership. They lost and the future 16th president of the USA moved with his parents to Indiana. Another well-known, but infamous visitor was Jesse James, once together with his brother Frank considered the most dangerous outlaws in the Wild West. After the Civil War (1861-1864) he formed the James Gang with a group of veterans from the Confederate Army. When things became too hot to handle, he went to Bardstown and hid in the tavern. The local sheriff at the time, Donnie Pence, was Jesse's cousin. The bullet-holes in the murals are said to have been caused by Jesse James, who mistook them for birds -probably after he had enjoyed a stiff drink or two in the bar.

In 1886 George Talbott bought the tavern, then known as Newman House. Together with his wife Annie, he expanded the tavern and turned it into a successful business. Their marriage bore fruit in the form of 12 children, of whom sadly only five survived childhood. When George died in 1912, his wife immortalized him by renaming the tavern Talbott Hotel.

The tavern is also the birthplace of a famous African American: Alexander Walters. He was one of the founders of the National Association for the Advancement of Colored People (NAACP), at its inception on February 12, 1909, still called The National Negro Committee. His mother worked as a slave in the kitchen and legend has it that she immediately resumed cooking again after having given birth to Alexander.

Around 1960 the tavern was further expanded with a west wing and in 1968 lawyer Jack Kelley III and three of his friends acquired the business. In 1981 Kelley bought them out. Consequently the Kelley family became the sole owner and felt responsible for preserving this historical building, also dubbed "the oldest stagecoach stop in America." Kelley's dedication to the tavern was illustrated after a severe fire that destroyed the entire interior of Talbott Tavern in 1998. Luckily the whole structure was not damaged beyond repair and Kelley decided to rebuild and restore the tavern. The insurance company covered some of the expenses, but the Kelley family had to contribute from their own pockets.

We can only be happy that they decided to rebuild, since a visit to this unique piece of American history is worthwhile. Not only lovers of bourbon, but also paranormalists enjoy coming to the tavern. During the night ghosts seem to appear, doors and windows open and close without assistance, key chains disappear from rooms and resurface downstairs in the bar, and light, colored spheres appear in bedrooms. Another ghost often sighted is the

White Lady, dressed in an 18th century gown, walking through the building.

Talbott Tavern today is managed by Jack Kelley, IV, with Jack Kelley, V waiting in the wings. Kelley is an enthusiastic bourbon adept and very knowledgeable about the subject. He gives his bartender room to assemble an impressive collection of different bourbons. Kelley invited us to taste a few of them when we visited the tavern some time ago. Proudly he showed us the list. I counted the bottles behind the bar and stopped at 60. Jack and I made a start with Knob Creek, named after the farm where Abe Lincoln grew up. After that, not necessarily in this order, we broadened our horizon with Michter's Single Barrel, Booker's, Rock Hill Farm, Russell's Reserve, Wild Turkey Rare Breed, Henry McKenna 10 Year Old, Ridgemont Reserve 1792, Wathens, Hancock Reserve and after that … I really don't know anymore. The next morning Becky, who wisely quit after three different bourbons, explained to me that she managed to get me to bed. I humbly bowed my head when breakfast was served. I too saw a spirit that night, but one from a bottle.

Bardstown is also famous for the Oscar Getz Museum of Whiskey History. It is named after a Chicago businessman who devoted his life to the liquor industry. Oscar Getz eventually became Chairman of the Board of Barton Distillers Associates, Inc, but was famous for collecting whisky paraphernalia from the 1930s on. He loved the heritage of the American bourbon history on the one hand but was a sound and modern businessman on the other.

Getz originally spread his collection over his house, his office and the Barton Distillery Museum in Bardstown, Kentucky. After his death in 1983 the museum was closed by the distillery. The management was of the opinion that the contents belonged to Getz personally and approached his widow Emma with the request to come up with a plan. She then decided to donate her late husband's collection to the city of Bardstown, together with a sum of money that would cover the startup of a small museum. As a result of her generosity the entire collection was put together in the historic Spalding Hall in Bardstown. On display is a unique collection of rare artifacts and documents about America's whiskey industry. They date from pre-Colonial days to post-Prohibition years. There are exhibits on President Washington and Abraham Lincoln, authentic moonshine stills, antique bottles and jugs, medicinal whiskey bottles and advertising art. The same building houses the Bardstown Historical Museum containing items from 200 years of local history, including various Indian relics, Lincoln documents, pioneer papers, a John Fitch land grant and a replica of his first steamboat, Stephen Foster memorabilia, gifts of Louis Philippe and Charles

***

A tavern filled with so many bourbons and a museum harboring a surprising variety of distilling artifacts, brings to mind a very special musician.

This man brought harmonica playing to a new level

altogether, as Sidney Bechet had done with the clarinet at the turn of the 19th century. He combined styles and collected guest appearances as varied as the bourbons on Talbot Tavern's shelves. A whole museum could be filled with pictures of him playing with the numerous musicians who enjoyed having him on stage. He was born as James Whiting, but he is far better known by his self-chosen nickname. His website explains as follows: "I needed a nickname... all the good ones were taken! You know 'Muddy Waters', 'Blind Lemon', 'Sonny Boy'...until one night a friend and I were leaving a concert - a Doc Watson concert - when somebody threw out of the window a box full of old 78s: I picked one up and it said "Sugar Blues" by Sidney Bechet... That's it! I thought it was perfect...so here I am..."

The quote on the website is accompanied by a picture of Sugar Blue standing next to Sidney Bechet's bust in New Orleans. It is not the only reference to jazz. Many others call Sugar Blue the Charlie Parker of the Blues Harp. His playing and singing encompass the whole domain of blues, jazz and beyond.

James Whiting was born on December 16, 1949 and grew up in Harlem, New York, among many professional musicians, his mother being a dancer and singer at the Apollo Theatre. At a young age he met Billy Holliday and instantly knew he wanted to become a performing musician too. When an aunt gave him a harmonica he started to practice by playing along with songs on the radio, ranging from Stevie Wonder to Dexter Gordon. He tried all kinds of instruments along the way, determined to go on stage himself sometime. Hearing Little Walter accompanying Muddy Waters pushed him over to the harmonica definitively. Listening to so many different musical styles gave him a sound basis for the completely unique and the very recognizable sound he would develop over the years.

He started playing the streets whenever he could but it was not until 1975 that he was first recorded with no less than guitarist Brownie McGhee and pianist Roosevelt Sykes. It meant the start of a career as a studio musician and soon he accompanied other great blues legends on their records, the likes of Johnny Shines who had played and toured with Robert Johnson in the 1930s, grand old blues lady Victoria Spivey, and another fine pianist, Memphis Slim. The latter advised Sugar Blue to move to Paris, France, to broaden his horizon. That move brought him world fame when he teamed up with the Rolling Stones. They were literally blown away by his sound and asked him to play on their *Some Girls* album. Now Sugar Blue could work on his studio career in Europe. But the Stones did more than that. They invited him on many concerts to play along with the band and even offered him an indefinite spot. But Sugar Blue was ready to make his next move, his own band, and refused.

Mick Jagger would comment about him, "He is a very strange and talented musician." Meanwhile Blue returned to Chicago and played with fellow harmonica players to learn even more. He spent time with Junior Wells, Cary Bell, Walter Horton and James Cotton. Instead of forming his own group he joined Willie Dixon's Chicago Blues All

Stars and toured with the enigmatic bass player, who was not only a friend but also a mentor to him. In the early 1980s they performed at North Sea Jazz in The Hague, and it was there where I heard him for the first time, together with my trusted Dutch harmonica friend Klaas, who would later that evening play backstage with Sugar Blue. A moment we both never forgot.

Finally in 1983 Sugar Blue assembled his own group. Ten years later, on his debut album *Blue Blazes*, for Alligator Records, he honored the Rolling Stones with his own rendition of "Miss You," the Jagger/Richards song where he played that recognizable riff. He has been touring the world with his band, appearing in America, Europe and Africa, sharing the stage with many, for over 25 years now. In the process he developed his singing and songwriting to a high level. He appeared in several movies among which *Johnny Handsome* and *Angel Heart* (with Robert DeNiro), where he also featured on Alan Parker's musical score.

The list of people he performed with is incredibly long and impressive. Indeed it looks like a museum collection of famous musicians and contains Bob Dylan, Hiram Bullock, Lonnie Brooks, Roosevelt Sykes, Melvin Taylor, Cary Bell, The Rolling Stones, Johnny B. Moore, Willie Dixon, Memphis Slim, Louisiana Red, Eddie Clearwater, Johnny Shines, Phish, Pinetop Perkins, Victoria Spivey, Son Seals, James Cotton, Frank Zappa, Big Walter Horton, Brownie McGhee, Bob Margolin, James Cotton, Muddy Waters, Art Blakey and Fats Domino.

His official website sums it all up beautifully, "Sugar Blue incorporates what he has learned into his visionary and singular style, technically dazzling yet wholly soulful. He bends, shakes, spills flurries of notes with simultaneous precision and abandon, combining dazzling technique with smoldering expressiveness and gives off enough energy to light up several city square blocks... And sings too! His distinctive throat tends to be overlooked in the face of his instrumental virtuosity - he's got a rich, sensual voice with a whisper of huskiness, which by itself would be something out of the ordinary. But oh, there's that harmonica again... !!"

What to sip with such a genius? I'd probably go for a beautifully crafted small batch bourbon called Ridgemont Reserve, created by Barton Brands. Listen to Blue's *From Chicago to Paris*. Both bourbon and album are multi-layered and very savory.

Talbott Tavern in the heart of Bardstown, Kentucky.

Whole Lotta Roses
Jim Rutledge and Stevie Ray Vaughan

Since 1992 both the Four Roses distillery and brand carry the same name, but in the foregoing 125 years they led separate lives. The question of how the name came into existence renders various stories. A closer look at this mellow, complex and tasty Kentucky Straight Bourbon Whiskey will reveal more. For that we have to travel back in time, to the first quarter of the 1800s.

In 1818 Joe Peyton built a small distillery on Gilbert's Creek, near the village of McBrayer, Anderson County, Kentucky. Step-by-step he expanded his little business and after a while decided to sell his Old Joe Distillery to a certain Mr. Hawkins. That was the starting point for a period in time that the distillery changed many hands, until 1909, when a severe fire destroyed more than 4,000 casks of whiskey, as well as the warehouses. In 1911 however Old Joe was rebuilt by a consortium and started producing whiskey again until Prohibition. When this disastrous period finally ended, the same consortium bought nearby Old Prentice Distillery and renamed it Old Joe Distillery. Soon after that the original Old Joe would only serve as a warehouse.

Old Prentice Distillery was built in 1855, also near McBrayer. It produced an eponymous whiskey until Prohibition. Soon after 1933 production restarted and the name of the distillery changed to ... yes, ... Old Joe. In 1942 Sam

Bronfman's Canadian Company Seagram's bought the distillery and renamed her Four Roses. Seagram already owned the brand name. At the time Four Roses whiskey was very popular. When Seagram, under management of the third generation Bronfman, sold its portfolio of drinks at the end of 2001, a Japanese company bought Four Roses. Since 19 February 2002 Kirin Brewing Ltd is the proud owner of brand and distillery.

Shortly after the Civil War (1861-1865), a trader in whiskey traveled in Tennessee and Georgia. His name was Paul Jones. Some 20 years later he arrived in Kentucky, having acquired the brand name Four Roses from the Rose family in Tennessee. Legend has it the family had four daughters, hence the brand name. Jim Rutledge, the current Master Distiller of Four Roses, tells another, more romantic version of the story, "Paul Jones proposed to a young southern lady and asked her to answer him at the next ball. She was to wear a corsage on her gown consisting of roses. Three would mean No, four would mean Yes. When she wore four roses at the ball, he decided to honor his beautiful wife, calling one of the whiskeys he traded Four Roses."

A fact is that the Paul Jones Company, who sold whiskey under the names Paul Jones Whiskey and Four Roses, bought Frankfort Distillers in 1922. The latter company, a conglomerate of small distillers, belonged to the small, exclusive group that was allowed to sell whiskey for medicinal purposes during Prohibition. This was the reason for Paul Jones Company's purchase in the first place...they needed it to continue the sales of Four Roses bourbon.

When Seagram's bought the distillery in 1942, Four Roses was the bestselling "post-Prohibition bourbon" in the USA. An excellent reason and time to name the distillery after the bourbon, but that was not the case. For years the distillery would operate under different names. Up until the mid 1980s it was called Old Prentice and in the late 1980s it was changed into Joseph E. Seagram Distillery, only to be baptized Four Roses Distillery in 1992. Well, whatever the name was after 1942, apart from Four Roses a lot of other bourbon was made at the distillery as a flavoring component for Seagram's blended whiskeys, most notably Seven Crown and Crown Royal.

At the end of the 1950s Four Roses sold over 200,000 cases per year of its Straight Kentucky Bourbon in the USA. To clarify: a case contains 12 bottles of .75 liters each, together 9 liters, which totals 1.8 million liters. Around 1960 Seagram found the domestic market was saturated and decided that the straight bourbon should only be sold in foreign markets, mainly Europe and Japan. For the home market Seagram switched to a blended version, containing at least 66% grain alcohol. This strategy delivered a bad name to Four Roses in its own back yard, where the new "yellow label" was positioned at the low-end of the market. At the same time Four Roses started to conquer Europe and East Asia with a beautiful, mellow, tasty straight Kentucky bourbon.

The afore-mentioned Jim Rutledge, more than 40 years active in the whisky industry, of which 35 years at Sea-

174

gram's, didn't like the change of strategy at all. He knew how good Four Roses' straight bourbon was and kept trying to convince Seagram to make the bourbon available for the US market again and get rid of the cheap blend. According to the marketing people that could not be done using the same label and packaging. That would only confuse the consumer. Jim, not one to give up easily, convinced the new owners, Kirin, that Four Roses Straight Kentucky Bourbon should be re-launched in the US under its old yellow label. To upgrade the brand name Jim introduced a single barrel version of Four Roses in 2004. It became an instant winner and this expression is readily available for the European and Japanese market as well. In September 2006, the intrepid distiller launched Four Roses Small Batch Bourbon. In the USA Four Roses quietly disassociated itself from the earlier unwanted image and re-established the true value of a beautiful, history-rich, mellow bourbon. A crown on Jim Rutledge's work was the election of the single barrel version as "Best American Whiskey under 10 Years Old" by *Whisky Magazine.*

Four Roses Distillery is housed in the buildings that were once Old Prentice. Its architecture is beautiful, although totally different from your standard Kentucky building. It more closely resembles a Mexican hacienda, complete with a bell in the wall, mounted above the main entrance. The entire premises are immaculately kept, complete with a beautiful visitor center and shop.

The mash tub is made of stainless steel and two different mash bills are used. The first one contains about 60%

corn, 35% rye and 5% malted barley; the second one 75%, 20% and 5% respectively. The grain source has not changed since the 1960s. Consistency is key in this place. American distillers value the role yeast places in the entire process much more than most of their Scottish counterparts. They grow their own yeast cultures, some of which have existed for over 100 years. At Four Roses five different strains are used. In combination with the two different mash bills it allows Jim and his team to create no less than 10 different flavors that all mature in different casks. The ten are used to create Four Roses Straight Kentucky Bourbon Whiskey by blending the casks. This method is unique to the distillery.

During our visit Jim Rutledge, Brent Elliott and Jota Tanaka, responsible for QA, offered us the possibility of sampling the different flavors. The tasting glasses were coded with four letters that are also used on the casks. The second letter defines the mash bill and the fourth letter the yeast strain. The S refers to former owner Seagram's. The result was an extraordinary olfactory experience. Under the interested and thoughtful eye of Jota-san we noted:

> OBSV - peppermint
> OESV - spicy
> OBSK - phenolic, spicy
> OESK - fruity
> OBSQ - floral
> OBSF - slightly minty and medicinal

The fermentation vessels are made of red cypress wood, but could eventually be replaced by stainless steel. According to Jim that will not affect the taste. It simply is more efficient in cleaning. It won't be his concern anymore. "These will last another lifetime" he laughed when asked. The beer still is made of copper. The fermented mash will be entirely distilled and then transported to the doubler, actually a pot still. A better name would be tripler, since Four Roses distills twice in the beer still, as Jim showed us on a model in the visitor center. Distilling three times in this manner is unique in the bourbon industry. Woodford Reserve triple distills as well, but solely using pot stills. The distillate, or white dog passes a so-called tailbox on its way to the receiver. At this stage in the process the alcohol percentage lawfully is not allowed to be higher than 160 proof (80% ABV).

Four Roses does not mature on-site, but in Cox Creek, Bullitt County, a 45-minute drive. All Four Roses spirit is filled into tankers and transported. Before it is poured into the casks the distillate has, again prescribed by law, to be diluted to at least 125 proof (62.5% ABV). The warehouses are low, only one storey, contrary to the "apartment build-ings" at other distilleries that are built up to seven stories. The casks are raised in two layers of three casks each and are not rotated. The top layer casks mature at about eight degrees F (4.5° C) difference from the ones on the bottom row. After maturation the casks are carefully selected and blended before bottling. Separate barrels are handpicked for the single barrel version.

177

Bottling takes place elsewhere at a central bottling plant. The bourbon for Europe is bottled in Scotland and product for Asia in Japan. Only the single barrel version is bottled on-site on a small flexible production line, manned by distillery retirees and relatives of the people that work daily at the distillery and warehouses. Filtration is applied since a lot of char residuals are in the cask, resulting from the fact that the casks are used for the first time. All casks for Four Roses are produced by Independent Staves, a nearby cooperage. The casks are heavily charred before use. During maturation 4.5% volume is lost each year, primarily caused by soakage that only occurs in new barrels and secondarily by evaporation. It seems the angels in the US are having a better time than the ones in Scotland, where the Angels' Share averages only 2.4%.

Every spring a special limited edition Single Barrel Bourbon is released and every autumn a similar Small Batch Bourbon appears. The casks for these editions are hand selected by the master distiller and have matured longer than the ones used for the standard bottlings. These limited expressions are only available for the US market. The brands Four Roses Super Premium and Fine Old Bourbon are exported exclusively to Japan. Maybe that's right. After all, Four Roses not only thanks its continued existence and revival to people like Jim Rutledge but also to the people of Kirin Brewery Ltd and the many, many Japanese consumers who have cherished and savored this excellent whiskey for a long time. They like the blues too, proven by the many concerts that have been recorded in Japan.

***

Jim Rutledge revived an old, historic brand, but put something else beside it, new expressions of the same brew. Subtle, captivating, full of soul and character. A young American guitarist did a similar thing. In a period when the blues suffered from less attention and tended to be overshadowed by the punk of the late 1970s and the synthesized pop of the early 1980s, a powerful album hit the charts. It came from Texas, where something had been brewing for almost 30 years. Now it was time to step up.

In 1983 Stevie Ray Vaughan brought back the focus on the electric blues and at the same time added new flavors to it, without forgetting where it all came from. He recorded the album *Texas Flood* with Tommy Shannon on bass and Chris "Whipper" Layton on drums. Their band Double Trouble instantly became famous. For SRV himself it didn't come overnight: he had been playing guitar since he was seven years old. Born in Dallas, Texas, on the third of October 1954, Stephen Ray, as he was officially named, grew up around many musicians in the Texas scene, not least his older brother Jimmy who would become famous with his Fabulous Thunderbirds in years to come. Other early influences were Jimi Hendrix, Lonnie Mack and Doyle Bramhall. The latter stimulated Stevie to develop skills as a singer and songwriter. At the age of 13 he formed his first band and a few years later was recorded for the first time during a sit in with a high school band. In 1970 he was ready to commit himself to music entirely, formed a new band called Blackbird and hit the road. They chose Austin, Texas as their base camp and began to play regular gigs in the city's Soap Creek Saloon. SRV was on the move! Two years later he teamed up with the rock group Krackerjack and joined forces with an old neighborhood friend, bass player Tommy Shannon. It didn't last long. Stevie was a stickler for "the real thing" and refused to wear theatrical make-up on stage, as was demanded by the lead singer. It didn't take long for him to make an appearance in another band, The Nightcrawlers. There he joined early childhood mentor Doyle Bramhall, who played the drums. They continued to work together, writing songs, even making some – unreleased – recordings in Hollywood. SRV returned to Austin, Texas and in 1974 joined yet another band, which was already very popular in the region.

This native Austin group of musicians was called Paul Ray and the Cobras. They were successful indeed, doing five shows a week, releasing a record and winning a regional award. For three years SRV shared the stage with Paul Ray. Then he formed a new band himself and called it Triple Threat Revue. With female vocalist Lou Ann Barton, SRV later renamed the band Double Trouble. The line-up changed a couple of times. Chris Layton replaced the first drummer and Tommy Shannon again showed up in SRV's musical life. The three-man band that would become famous in just two years began to take form. Shannon had been playing and touring with Johnny Winter for quite some time and had been tutored in the blues by the white haired guitar wizard for years.

It was drummer Charlie Watts who picked up a tape and after listening to it, invited them to a party for the Rolling Stones in New York. There were many musicians in the crowd and Double Trouble started jamming with some of them. Among those were Jackson Browne and David Bowie. The latter asked SRV to come and play in the studio for his album *Let's Dance* and liked it so much that he asked SRV to join him on the *Serious Moonlight* tour. It didn't work out for similar reasons as with Krackerjack. Stevie didn't want to become part of a theatrical act, preferring to play the real blues with his buddies Layton and Shannon. He accepted an invitation from Jackson Browne to come record in his LA-studio for free. At the threshold of 1982 the first recordings for what was to become the *Texas Flood* album were made. When legendary talent scout and record producer John Hammond heard an earlier live recording from Double Trouble, the man with the "golden ear" stepped in and signed Double Trouble with Epic. So, when SRV hit the charts with his debut album in 1983, he had been preparing himself for 16 years. Within two years another two albums hit the charts, *Couldn't Stand the Weather* and *Soul to Soul*. The former gave a demonstration of SRV's deep connection with and love for Jimi Hendrix. If ever "Voodoo Chile" was covered in a way that would have satisfied Hendrix, it must be this rendition. The latter album featured a new, fourth band member, keyboard player Reese Wynans.

The fourth album was a live record, released in 1986. Musically everything went well but on a personal level SRV went through a rough period. His father Big Jim Vaughan died in autumn that year and Stevie collapsed. The years of drugs and alcohol abuse caught up with him. Fortunately he found strength in his religion and in his old time friend Tommy Shannon. They went into rehab at the same time, albeit in different cities.

Both resurfaced sober within the year and recorded what Shannon calls their best album ever, *In Step*. Double Trouble continued to pick up prizes and compliments. In the following years many contemporary musicians would share the stage with the threesome, among whom Albert Collins, B.B. King, Albert King, Paul Butterfield, Chaka Khan and Joe Cocker.

In 1990 Double Trouble went on tour with Eric Clapton. After having played their second show on August 26, in the Alpine Valley Music Theatre, East Troy, Wisconsin, fate struck SRV's last chord on earth. The helicopter that was supposed to fly him to the next gig crashed into a nearby mountain, due to a dense fog and the pilot's unfamiliarity with the terrain. Tommy Shannon and Chris Layton were not on board, but several of Clapton's crewmembers were. All died instantly.

Five days later, Stevie Ray Vaughan's funeral service was held in Dallas, Texas. Many blues musicians were present to pay a final honor to a formidable guitar player and songwriter, who, according to Tommy Shannon, always wanted to help other people and continued to believe in "the real thing" his entire life. He would be honored posthumously in various ways, among others with a statue in

Austin, Texas, standing on the borders of Lady Bird Lake, an SRV Memorial Scholarship Fund and many blues songs by artists the likes of Jimmy Vaughan, Buddy Guy and Steve Vai. Bonnie Raitt dedicated her 1991 album *Luck of the Draw* to him and Stevie Wonder immortalized him in 1995, while performing *Stevie Ray Blues*. The great B.B. King is a huge fan of SRV and might have given him the greatest compliment of all, when he once said, "I always thought that you had to be double black to play the blues, until I heard Stevie Ray Vaughan play and realized he was neither."

SRV had a lifelong love affair with the Fender Stratocaster, not surprisingly so, since Albert "The Master of the Stratocaster" Collins and Jimi Hendrix were among his strongest influences. He played various Fenders and had nicknames for them, like Number One, Charley, Lenny (after his first wife), Butter, Main and Yellow.

The latter name reminds me of the yellow label and mellow character of the original Four Roses Straight Kentucky Bourbon. When I take a sip of that one, my first bourbon ever, I almost immediately hear SRV play "Tin Pan Alley." For me the subtleness, the development and the character in both is almost second to none.

Four Roses' copper doubler.

A tanker with white dog on its way to the barrel filling station.

Payin' the Cost to Be the Boss
James C. Crow and B.B. King

Situated amidst the world-famous horse farms of Kentucky, with owners such as Queen Elisabeth II, is a typical, well-preserved little American town. It dates back to
the late 19th century and is named after the colossal pal-
ace of the French monarch Louis XIV aka The Sun King:
Versailles, articulated locally something like "for sale." In
this town starts the history of Woodford Reserve, the only
triple pot distilled bourbon in the USA. The stills used are
genuinely Scottish, built by Forsyth's from Rothes, Speyside. Full circle, because it was the Scotsman James Crow
who showed the original owner's son the way.

The 4th of July 1776 was that glorious day on which
the Americans freed themselves from the yoke of the British. The USA was born. Elijah Pepper, born in 1775, founded a small, healthy distillery in Versailles, Kentucky, at the
time still part of Virginia, in 1797. He called his baby Old
Pepper Springs. Within four years Pepper's whiskey was
widely known in the region. Pepper was so successful that
he was one of the few distillers able to afford the high
taxes that had caused the Whiskey Rebellion in 1794. Most
farmers in the neighborhood could not finance the tax
payments and brought their corn surplus to Pepper, who
turned it into whiskey. Business kept growing and Pepper
had to expand. In 1812 he found the ideal spot: Grassy
Springs, a branch of Glenn's Creek, north of Versailles.

Until his death in 1831 Elijah Pepper stayed true to his calling: making small batches of high quality bourbon. His son Oscar succeeded him and decided in 1833 to employ the Scottish scientist and chemist Dr. James C. Crow. During the next 22 years Crow dedicated himself to improving and optimizing the distillation process. He developed a series of measuring instruments that were almost immediately taken on by other distilleries. In the area of process hygiene Crow also made waves. He experimented with charred barrels to influence the maturation and in doing so created a standard that is used by every current-day distillery. Crow is responsible for the fact that Pepper's whiskey became better and much more consistent in quality, by inventing the sour mash method. This term refers to the residue in the mash tub from the previous batch. Some of it is added to the next batch to distill, thus creating consistency. Fame rose high for the small distillery in Glen Creek and its whiskey boasted many celebrity-fans, including president Andrew Jackson and writer Mark Twain.

When Crow died in 1856, he left an indelible stamp on bourbon distilling. Oscar Pepper met his Maker in 1865. His son James was 14 years old then, too young to succeed his father. The first years after Oscar's death, young James was assisted by banker Edmund H. Taylor, who in due time became famous with the Bottle-in-Bond Act (1897). Taylor rebuilt the distillery in 1874. James Pepper seems to have been better in drinking the product than selling it. Around 1878 he was in dire financial straits and had no other choice than to sell the very famous distillery to whiskey

merchants Leopold Labrot and James Graham. They expanded the distillery, but kept the traditional ways of producing whiskey. In a time when most distillers converted
to multi-storied warehouses "Old Pepper Distillery, Labrot
& Graham Proprietors" stayed true to the belief that small,
stone warehouses with thick walls matured the whiskey
better than the new high steel constructions.

Like many of its colleagues and competitors, L&G
couldn't avoid being closed during Prohibition. Moving
their stock to Frankfort Distillers they managed to continue selling whiskey "for medicinal purposes only." In 1933
L&G restarted production. Seven years later Brown-Forman
from Louisville (the current owner of Jack Daniel's) sought
expansion possibilities and, in order to meet the increasing
demand for bourbon, acquired L&G for $75,000, including
an option on the 25,763 barrels of maturing whiskey. A
bargain!

In the mid 1960s the small boutique-like distilleries
lost their charm to the big conglomerates and Brown-
Forman decided to close the distillery in Glen Creek. In
1972 Brown-Forman sold the property to Freeman Hockensmith, keeping an option to buy it back if the new owner
decided to put it up for sale again. Hockensmith concentrated on producing gasohol as a substitute for car fuel. It
was the time of the worldwide oil crisis. When the crisis
was over, about a year later, the demand for gasohol dried
up and the distillery was mothballed again. In the next
23 years nature claimed back what man had developed in
Glen Creek. The buildings suffered vandalism and slowly

but surely became overgrown with weeds and ivy. In 1994 Hockensmith died and Brown-Forman used its option to buy back the property. The large drinks company subsequently spent $10.5 million in a historical restoration project that eventually delivered a showpiece distillery, with all old traditions being kept alive. Brown-Forman noted the increasing interest in whiskey tourism and applied for status as an Historic Landmark, which was soon granted. In 1996 after almost a quarter of a century, stills ran again in Glen Creek. In 2003 the name of the distillery - and the whiskey - was officially changed to Woodford Reserve. It has become The Showcase in the American whiskey industry, thanks to Brown-Forman.

Woodford Reserve Distiller's Select Kentucky Straight Bourbon Whiskey is bottled in numbered batches at 90.4 proof (45.2% ABV) at a minimum age of six years. The color is beautiful: amber-gold. The nose is sweet with hints of vanilla and honey. The taste is complex with citrus fruit, spices and flowers in a good balance. The aftertaste is long, spicy and smooth. For VIP's and for the Kentucky Derby special editions are bottled, containing the same whiskey as the standard bottling. In 2005 Woodford Reserve introduced the Masters Collection, special whiskeys in limited stocks. The first two were the called the Four Grain and had a mash bill that slightly differed from the standard one, since it also contained wheat. The yeast strain also differed from the standard expression. The next in the series was the Sonoma-Cutrer Finish, extra-matured in California chardonnay wine barrels. Technically this could not

189

be called bourbon. More recent expressions include the 1838 Sweet Mash and the Seasoned Oak Finish.

The region of Kentucky where Woodford Reserve has been crafted originally belonged to Virginia, only becoming part of another state in 1792. The many French names in the region, like Versailles, Frankfort and Louisville, not only reflect the French influence but also are a gesture of thanks to the French king of the House of Bourbon for his assistance in fighting the British during the Revolutionary War. A whole county was even named after the French Royal Family: Bourbon County! Although currently all Kentucky distilleries are located outside that county, the name sticks to the product. Nowadays 95% of all American whiskey may still be called bourbon.

***

A showpiece of a distillery, with all old traditions being kept alive. Similar words apply to B.B. King who can easily be dubbed the show master of the blues, with all traditions kept alive indeed. Like Woodford Reserve combines the best of Scottish distilling tradition with American skills and grains, B.B. King has incorporated different musical styles into his music, ranging from rock 'n' roll, jazz, swing, funk and soul, to down-home blues. Like so many blues men, King originates from the Delta where he was born in Itta Bena on September 16, 1925 and baptized Riley B. King. He grew up helping his sharecropper parents and joined a local gospel group, grooming his voice that would over time become one of the, if not *the* most recognizable in the history of the blues. Riley worked the fields for years, and from the age of 12, when he came into possession of a guitar, would play and sing whenever he had the chance. He didn't plan to leave the region, but in 1946 he accidentally drove a tractor into a barn on the plantation where he and his family worked. Afraid of being punished he ran away to Memphis, in search of his uncle Booker "Bukka" White who had already made a name for himself as a recorded blues artist. He took his young nephew in for a while and taught him some tricks on the guitar. Riley King didn't succeed in following in the footsteps of Bukka and returned to Mississippi, apologizing for what he had done and paying off his debt. Two years later Riley returned to Memphis and was helped by Sonny Boy Williamson II to get a job as a disc jockey at WDIA, an R&B Radio Station. This job earned him his nickname B(eale Street) B(luesboy) King and one year later he boasted his first recordings for the RPM label.

B.B. King was influenced by various musicians, but T-Bone Walker might have been the most important one, next to Louis Jordan with his jump blues. T-Bone's playing made him realize he had to switch from acoustic to electric guitar. Soon he formed his own band and started touring the circuit. And that meant heavy touring. In 1956, B.B. King accomplished a groundbreaking record of 342 booked gigs. This year also marked the foundation of Blues Boys Kingdom, his own record label. Regardless of his constant touring he managed to record many hits and would become one of the foremost R&B artists ever. With his hit "The Thrill is Gone," arranged as a crossover between blues and pop, he gained a whole new audience in the pop crowd and a Grammy in 1971. Europe had picked him up rapidly in the blues revival of the 1960s and King could be seen performing all over the old continent. When back in the USA he was asked to open for the Rolling Stones US Tour of 1969. Meanwhile he kept performing approximately 250 concerts a year, a habit that cost him both his marriages. At the end of the 1980s he again spoke to a new crowd of listeners when he worked with U2 to record *Rattle and Hum.* Consequently he shared the stage with them on their tour.

B.B. King was inducted into the Blues Hall of Fame in 1980. His discography reads like a catalog of blues and related music and the awards he received over time are numerous, among which 15 Grammies and the Presidential Medal of Freedom. King is known for remembering his roots and honoring them when possible. In Memphis, where he started his career as a disc jockey he opened his first B.B. King's Blues Club in 1991. The second one opened three years later in Los Angeles – the one where I happened to hear Eric Sardinas - that formidable guitarist, so heavily influenced by Johnny Winter, but firmly holding his own ground – the same year. Six more clubs would follow in years to come. The King is known for his philanthropy as well. Among other functions he is an honorary board member of Little Kids Rock, a non-profit organization that provides musical instruments to public schools in need

At the turn of the 20th century, the all-round perform-er of the blues appeared in the 2000 sequel to the *Blues Brothers* movie and a few years later he worked with Eric Clapton. *Riding with the King* is the audible result of that cooperation. B.B. King has influenced a whole plethora of blues musicians and is continuing to do so.

He will not leave the spotlights lightly it seems. He tried to say goodbye to the stage in 2006 when a Euro-pean farewell tour was organized, but kept reappearing in the UK, the Netherlands and even in South America in the following years. In 2009 a Brazilian journalist wanted to know if this was really his "last" farewell tour and B.B. King, known for his humor on stage, reportedly answered, "One of my favorite actors is a man from Scotland named Sean Connery. Most of you know him as James Bond, 007. He made a movie called *Never Say Never Again.*"

He shares his love of a special type of guitar with Ste-vie Ray Vaughan, albeit that B.B. King prefers a special black Gibson called Lucille. There is a famous story at-tached to that name. In the days back in the Delta, he once performed in a juke joint, where a fight broke out and a fire started. Everybody fled, including B.B., who suddenly realized his precious guitar was still inside. He ran back into the building, grabbed his instrument and managed to jump outside, just before the joint collapsed. Only later he found out that the fight was over a woman called Lucille. To remind himself of his foolishness in jeopardizing his life, then and there he decided to call his guitar Lucille.

Scotsman James Crow once learned distilling in the old country and was generous to share it with pioneers having become rebels, turning into Americans. He improved the distillation process significantly and many of his inventions and improvements are still used in today's whiskey industry.

B.B. King learned to play in the Delta, and later shared the stage generously with many American and European musicians. By doing so he improved the acceptance of the blues, the sharing of the music between people, regardless their origins.

Crow was a craftsman to the hilt and laid the foundation for Woodford Reserve, which honors the tradition of distilling bourbon and at the same time embraces innovation. He was constantly trying to perfect the process. B.B. King is a craftsman too, still showing the tradition of the blues, whilst carrying it into new dimensions and still continuing to play whenever he can. I salute you both.

Because the thrill of feisty blues and a savory bourbon on the side will probably never leave me, I cannot resist advising you to listen to B.B.'s greatest hit with the taste of Woodford Reserve in the background. So here we go, one more time: *Thrill is Gone.*

Woodford Reserve is triple distilled in Scottish copper pot stills.

THE ENCORE

It Ain't Bourbon and It Ain't Blues
Jack Daniel and Keith Richards

An American whiskey that cannot be called bourbon. A founder who was born two years after his mother died. Favorite tipple of rock-icon Keith Richards for many years. A little town with an irresistible 19th century charm. World championship BBQ and a vast horde of hardcore fans from all over the world. A nice list of ingredients to party. Let's begin with the man who gave his name to the best selling whiskey in the world.

Jack Daniel's grave is topped with a roughly finished stone marker, a symbol for his untimely death at the age of 61. According to many, his life was only half-built. The ladies of Lynchburg mourned heavily over the loss of the life-long bachelor, who supposedly had many mistresses. The men, on the contrary, seemed happy at the funeral.

Reading his tombstone, one can safely surmise that Jack Daniel lived from 1850 until 1911. A straightforward miracle, since his mother's tombstone, at a nearby family cemetery, reveals her death to be in 1848. Ben Green, a journalist who wrote the biography *Jack Daniel's Legacy* in 1967, mentions that Jasper Newton Daniel was born on September 5, 1846 and that his mother died five months after she delivered him, in 1847. Confusion all around! When I ask Candy Richard, with whom we stayed in a B&B a couple of miles west of Lynchburg, she answered, as if she had personally known him, "Jack was very vain!"

Jasper "Jack" Newton Daniel indeed left home when, according to journalist Ben Green, he was six years old, because "I am afraid of my stepmother." In 2004 Peter Krass contradicted that story in his book *Blood and Whiskey*, stating that Jack must have been 15 when he left his parents' home. Whatever is true, Jack was a youngster when he came to live with "Uncle" Felix Waggoner, an elderly, gentleman farmer in the area and neighbor of the Daniels. After a couple of years Waggoner arranged for Jack to work at Dan Call's farm. Call was a prosperous farmer and part-time preacher, who ran a small whiskey still in a barn at his farm. He recognized the zeal in the boy and asked one of his slaves, Nearest Green, to teach Jack the art of distilling so that he could become "the best whiskey maker in the world." When Call had to choose between being a minister and a whiskey distiller, he decided to give preaching a higher priority than distilling. In his absence Jack Daniel took care of the whiskey-business. His commercial instinct, his zest for being recognized, his charm and his temper would become the pillars that founded his whiskey-empire to be. Unfortunately one of these pillars also caused his untimely death. Jack died of the consequences of an infection in his big toe, as a result of kicking his safe when it wouldn't open. Stubbornly he didn't pay too much attention to it, which led first to amputation and gangrene in the end.

Under further pressure from his congregation, Dan Call had to stop distilling and sold his still in 1860 to Jack, who was either 14 (Green) or 18 (Krass) at the time. Dur-

200

ing the Civil War, Jack Daniel distilled and sold whiskey continuously in the area surrounding Lynchburg. In 1866 he joined forces with Colonel Hughes, but that lasted less than a year. As the sole proprietor he expanded his distilling business, bought land in Lynchburg and moved the distillery to The Hollow at Cave Spring in Lincoln County, which would become Moore County in 1872. Legend has it that Alfred Eaton, inventor of the Lincoln County Process, had already distilled whisky at The Hollow because of its clear limestone-filtered spring water.

Around 1880 Jack engaged his nephew Lem Motlow, a real go-getter, who would run the entire operation a few years later. Jack, Lem and the latter's brother Frank also erected The Farmer's Bank, partly to finance their expansion. This bank still exists and can be found on a corner of the picturesque village square of Lynchburg.

In 1909 Moore County was declared "dry" by law, way before Prohibition became a national item. Lem Motlow didn't hesitate a moment and moved distilling operations to St. Louis, Missouri and built a second distillery in Birmingham, Alabama, a couple of years later. During that period Jack Daniel officially could not be named Tennessee whiskey, and with Prohibition even those stills had to shut down. Moore County stayed dry after Prohibition and Jack Daniel's distillery in The Hollow was not allowed to resume production. Lem Motlow fought for what he weighed in pounds and eventually was granted permission to distill at Lynchburg again in 1938. Jack Daniel's was a real Tennessee whiskey again. When Lem died in 1947, his four sons, Reagor, Hap, Connor and Robert, took over the management of the distillery.

Around 1956 the worldwide demand for this whiskey was so huge - partly because many celebrities in the music and movie world drank Jack Daniel's and showed it, partly because the whiskey had won several prizes in international competitions - that the financial liquidity of the company became a problem. The company structure, with the many Motlow heirs, was not a healthy one business-wise. Brown-Forman, an old and respected drinks and distilling company from Louisville, Kentucky, came to the rescue and bought Jack Daniel Distillery for $18 million. The new owner honored the heritage of the company and appointed Reagor Motlow to its Board of Directors. His brothers stayed on as managers, illustrating the Southern maxim "if it ain't broke, don't fix it." Today the label still states: Lem Motlow, Proprietor. That honor befits the man who built Jack Daniel's into a worldwide brand.

When Jack Daniel started out as an independent whiskey merchant and distiller, he sold his whiskey under the brand names Belle of Lincoln and Old Fashioned. After some time he decided to change the name to Jack Daniel's Old No. 7. The origins of that name led to many speculations. Did it point to Jack's seven mistresses? He is supposed to have had many more than that. Did it refer to the seven barrels that were chalk-marked with a "7" and were accidentally delivered to a bar? The customers enjoyed that whiskey so much, that they kept asking for No. 7…

Or was it because of the re-numbering of counties and

distilleries in 1871? (according to Peter Krass, that is the real story). Did Jack Daniel want to emphasize with "Old No. 7" that he had made whiskey before 1871? Or did the whiskey age seven years? It is a well-known fact that JD is currently bottled between four and six years of maturation. According to Ben Green, the only true story is the one about Jack meeting a business-friend in Tullahoma who ran a chain of seven stores operating under his surname. Jack is supposed to have told that story after his visit at Tullahoma to his then-Master Distiller Bill Hughes. The latter's daughter, Mrs. Frank Parker, told this story to Ben Green in 1967.

Every step in the production process is done in or immediately around Lynchburg, on two different locations. The mash bill of Jack Daniel's states: 80% corn (from Illinois and Indiana), 8% rye (from Minnesota) and 12% malted barley (produced in Wisconsin from grain grown in Minnesota and North Dakota).

Although more than 51% corn is used and the whiskey matures in new charred oak barrels, Jack Daniel's is not allowed to call itself bourbon. That is because the whiskey is filtered through sugar maple charcoal, by which its taste is changed remarkably. This practice is often referred to as "charcoal mellowing." The official name is Lincoln County Process, and it distinguishes Tennessee Whiskey from bourbon. The other whiskey distillery in Lincoln County, George Dickel in Tullahoma (about 10 miles from Lynchburg), uses a similar process.

The mash is distilled twice in a column still to 140

proof (70% ABV) after which the spirit is filtered through a 10-foot thick layer of sugar maple charcoal. It is assumed that Mr. Eaton started this process to mellow the raw spirit slightly. Filtering takes up to four days, because the white dog literally trickles through the thick layer of charcoal. Every six months the layer is replaced by a new one made from the charcoal of 30 ricks of sugar maple. Planks of wood are stacked into a rick and burned carefully to charcoal at the rickyard. The used charcoal is sold to consumers as barbecue fuel. After filtering, the whiskey is poured into new oak barrels at 125 proof (62.5% ABV). The barrels are charred before use at a temperature of 1500° F (815.5° C), for 15 seconds. When the barrels are emptied after several years of maturing, the equivalent of two liters of charcoal comes out with the whiskey.

The whiskey in the famous square bottle with the black-and-white label matures four to six years in one of the 76 warehouses, located a few miles south of the distillery. One of the newer ones can hold approximately 45,000 barrels. The older ones, especially the ones that were build before 2000, can "only" hold 20,000. All whiskey is bottled at this location, where seven separate bottling lines run five days a week. One of them is dedicated to miniature bottles. Yearly about 10 million cases are shipped to 150 different countries. The total amounts to an annual output of 90 million liters. Almost 50% of it is shipped to Europe.

Lynchburg, Tennessee (pop. 361) reads the label on a bottle of Jack Daniel's. That might have been the case when the town came into being, around 1818. Around that time a lot of thieves were roaming about and a committee of "vigilant civilians" maintained the order. Many a thief was lynched around a big tree, hence the expression that Judge Lynch held court that particular day. Another legend tells that a weak man called Lynch always had to flog the convicts. Whatever story may be true, the town was named after the old ways of justice and punishment. In 1873 Lynchburg was officially chosen as the county seat for Moore County, which was created in 1871 out of parts of the counties Lincoln, Franklin, Coffee and Bedford. Today in and around Lynchburg approximately 5,000 people live. They work at the distillery, in the tourist industry and as farmers. During the annual World Championship Invitational Barbecue, the number of people staying in the area grows to an astonishing 30,000.

The tiny town center still looks as if it were the 19th century, apart from modern cars parked around the red brick courthouse. One can encounter real characters who have been living in and around Lynchburg their entire life. Farmer Woody Bedford for instance, who once said to us, when his distant cousin Jimmy Bedford was still at JD's helm, " Jimmy might be the master distiller over here, but I am the master consumer." Or the afore-mentioned Candy Richard, who shows up with a horse and buggy, offering tours through the neighborhood. Or the vivacious beautiful redheaded Bonnie Lewis who ran the annual BBQ for years, combining the task with being editor of the Moore County News. She now runs a gift shop, helped part time by her husband Randall who also works as a bonds man and is an accomplished guitarist with his own studio and band. No wonder we ended up with them, staying in their wonderful home, jammin' to the blues in the cellar on drums, guitar and vocals, while Bonnie served us Lynchburg Lemonade!

***

As mentioned in the introduction, in the early 1980s in my spare time I did the lighting and sound for the blues band of my friend Klaas, the harmonica player. The drummer of the band was a Keith Richards fan and he emulated his hero to a T, including his drinking habits. The drummer told me the lead guitar player of the Rolling Stones always kept a bottle of Jack Daniel's within reach and he pointed at his base drum. Inside, surrounded by the soundproofing material, there was a square bottle with a black label and white letters: Jack Daniel's Sour Mash Whiskey, Lynchburg, Tennessee. In hindsight, the seed for *Bourbon & Blues* was sown almost 30 years ago. At the time I thought JD was a bourbon. When I started to correspond with the distillery they soon corrected that mistake.

Keith Richards, one of the founding fathers of the Rolling Stones, whose name comes from a Muddy Waters song, is undoubtedly one of the huge celebrities in the world of rock, together with Mick Jagger, his musical all-time partner and co-founder of the Stones. How different would the history of rock 'n' roll have been if the Richards family had been home on July 5, 1944, when Keith was still a baby. A German V1 bomb destroyed their apartment when they

were away. At a young age Keith's mother let him listen
to jazz and blues records, providing him with a guitar as
well. His father didn't seem to like it as he was quoted as
one time yelling, "stop that bloody noise." As a thank you
for that Keith Richards confessed many years later, after
his father had been cremated, that he had snorted a bit of
his ashes. As a youngster Keith knew Mick Jagger, since
they went to the same primary school, but it was not until
1961 that they started to play together in a band called
Little Boy Blue and the Blue Boys, the forerunner of what
would become the Rolling Stones.

One of Keith Richards's earliest guitar influences was
Chuck Berry, who continued to inspire him. The Blue Boys
covered many songs that Berry had composed. Mick Jagger shared Keith's preference for Berry, Muddy Waters and
Bo Diddley. It would prove to be the foundation on which
the duo built the unique Rolling Stones sound. Their first
#1 Hit "I Can't Get No Satisfaction" is directly taken from
Muddy Waters title "I Can't Be Satisfied."

Keith Richards is most famous for his original rhythm
guitar playing but he can also sing, a skill he learned as a
boy when selected for the school choir. It delivered him his
"first taste of show biz" when he performed as a boy soprano in Westminster Abbey for Queen Elizabeth II. During
concerts Richards regularly takes a lead vocal with a few
songs. He is fairly modest about his voice and once said,
"It's not the most beautiful voice in the world anymore,
but the Queen liked it, when it was at its best...It's not been
my job, singing, but to me, if you're gonna write songs,

you've got to know how to sing." He also played bass on various Stones recordings, masters the keyboards and is responsible for producing many of their albums, together with Jagger, under their pseudonym The Glimmer Twins.

Keith Richards's musical ability is often overshadowed by his image as a drug abuser, an "honor" he earned in his early days with the Stones, when he was busted for drugs possession both in the UK and in Canada. However, he has never been shy about his substance abuse and the variety of it, which stamped him as the ultimate rock 'n' roll art-ist. Fellow musicians describe him as the musical leader of the Greatest Rock Band in the World, whereas he himself describes his role as "oiling the machinery."

Regardless of his drinking and drugs habits he is co-responsible for a long list of hit songs that are marinated in the blues but lean more towards rock 'n' roll, among which Buddy Holly's "Not Fade Away" and the original Jag-ger/Richards compositions "Jumpin' Jack Flash" and "It's only Rock & Roll (but I Like It)". And along the way Jack Daniel became part of his entourage.

Try sippin the Old No. 7 while listening to some (Sym-pathy for the) Devil Music. Or try a Jumpin' Gentleman Jack Flash with Aretha Franklin, for a smoother version. So what about that Devil Music and Holy Blues stuff?

Keith Richards summed it up nicely when he said: "There's only one song, and Adam and Eve wrote it; the rest is a variation on a theme."

Well, this ain't bourbon and it ain't blues but it sure tastes good!

The rick yard at Jack Daniel's; charcoal is made for filtering the white dog.

Some home-grown blues.

Do Try This at Home!

Early 1971, blues aficionado Bruce Iglauer left his paid job at Delmark Records to fully concentrate on his fledgling company Alligator Records, named after Bruce's habit of clicking his teeth when he enjoyed a particular song or artist. When still at Delmark he had recorded Hound Dog Taylor in the evening hours, since he couldn't convince his boss to sign up Hound Dog. Alligator was born and basically was a one-man-one-record-one artist company for nine months. Then Iglauer decided to quit Delmark and dedicate himself to his reptile record company full time. For the next few years Iglauer ran Alligator from his tiny apartment, filled with stacks of records and a shipping table next to his bed. Since he had a genuine aptitude for discovering blues talents, Iglauer's records won recognition by a larger crowd and slowly the company began to grow, contracting big names like Walter Horton, Lonnie Brooks, Albert Collins, Koko Taylor, Lonnie Mack, Johnny Winter, Buddy Guy, Clarence "Gatemouth" Brown, Son Seals, Magic Slim, Left Hand Frank, Sugar Blue, Carey Bell, Lil' Ed and the Blues Imperials, Charlie Musselwhite, Clifton Chenier, Coco Montoya and Shemekia Copeland, Johnny Copeland and Robert Cray. Bruce Iglauer has launched more than 300 records in almost 40 years. He has a complete office now with employees, but never forgets that indeed he did try this at home first!

I invite you to go to your own music collection and honor this remarkable man. Pull out a sample of the many goods that Alligator Records has to offer. And do pick your own bourbon to accompany these blues greats, preferably one that was matured in a barrel with alligator char. Have fun!

THE SCORES

You Can't Judge a Book by the Cover
A Bibliography with Bo Diddley

Books

Baraka, Amiri and Amina Baraka – *The Music* – Reflections on Jazz and Blues. William Morrow and Company Inc. 1987. ISBN 0688043887.

Baraka, Amiri (aka Leroi Jones) – *Blues People* – Morrow Quill Paperbacks 1963. ISBN 9780688184742.

Campbell, Sally van Winkle – *But Always Fine Bourbon* – Old Rip van Winkle Distillery 2004. ISBN 0967420806.

Cecil, Sam – *The Evolution of the Bourbon Whisky Industry in Kentucky* – Turner Publishing Company 2001. ISBN 1563114860.

Charters, Samuel – *The Roots of the Blues* – Marion Boyars Inc. 1981. ISBN 071452705X.

Cohn, Lawrence – *Nothing but the Blues, the Music and the Musicians* – Abbeville Press Publishers 1993. ISBN 1558592717

Cone, James H. – *The Spirituals and the Blues* – Orbis Books 1992. Originally published in 1972 by The Seabury Press.

Cowdery, Chuck – *Bourbon, Straight* – Made and Bottled in Kentucky 2004. ISBN 0975870300.

Evans, David – *Big Road Blues: Tradition and Creativity in the Folk Blues* - Dacapo 1987. ISBN 0520034848.

Getz, Oscar – *Whiskey, An American Pictorial History* – David McKay Company Inc. 1978. No ISBN. Library of Congress Catalog Card Number 78-55552.

Giola, Ted – Delta Blues – *The Life and Times of the Mississippi Masters Who Revolutionized American Music* – W.W. Norton & Company Inc. 2008. ISBN 9780393062588.

Givens, Ron – *Bourbon at Its Best* - Menasha Ridge Press/ Publishers Group West 2008. ISBN 9781578603046.

Graves, Tom – *Crossroads: The Life and Afterlife of Blues Legend Robert Johnson* – DeMers Books 2008. ISBN 9780981600215.

Green, Ben – *Jack Daniel's Legacy* - Published by the author 1967. No ISBN.

Kane, Frank – *Anatomy of the Whisky Business* – Lakehouse Press 1965. No ISBN.

Krass, Peter - *Blood & Whiskey, The Life and Times of Jack Daniel* - John Wiley & Sons 2004. ISBN 0471273929.

Lomax, Alan – *The Land Where the Blues Began* – Pantheon Books 1993. ISBN 0679404244.

Murray, Jim - *Classic Bourbon, Tennessee & Rye Whiskey* - Prion Books Limited 1998. ISBN 1853752185.

O'Neil, Jim and Amy van Singel (editors) –*The Voice of the Blues, Classic Interviews from Living Blues Magazine* – Routledge Taylor & Frances Group 2002. ISBN 0415936543.

Owens, Bill and Alan Dikty – *The Art of Distilling Whiskey and Other Spirits* – Quarry Books 2009. ISBN 9781592535699.

Pacult, F. Paul - *American Still Life* - John Wiley & Sons 2003. ISBN 0471444073.

Palmer, Robert – *Deep Blues* – MacMillan 1982. ISBN 0333340396.

Pearce, John Ed – *Nothing Better in the Market* – Brown Forman Distillers 1970. No ISBN. Library of Congress Catalog Card Number 76-110212.

Regan, Gary and Mardee Haidin Regan – *The Book of Bourbon* - Chapters Publishing Ltd. 1995. ISBN 1881527891.

Ripani, Richard J. – *The New Blue Music–Changes in Rhythm & Blues, 1950-1999* – University Press of Mississippi 2006. ISBN 1578068622.

Rowley, Matthew B. – *Moonshine!* - Lark Books 2007. ISBN 1 57990 648 6.

Samuels, Jr., Bill - *My Autobiography* - Maker's Mark - Saber Publishing 200. ISBN 0970586108.

Taylor, Richard – *The Great Crossing* – Buffalo Trace Distillery 2002. ISBN 097168319.

Trynka, Paul – *Portrait of the Blues* – Reed International Books Ltd 1996. ISBN 0306807793.

Wardlow, Gayle Dean – *Chasin' That Devil Music* – Backbeat Books 1998. ISBN 0879305525.

Waymack, Mark and James F. Harris – *The Book of Classic American Whiskeys* – Open Court Publishing Company 1995. ISBN 081269306X

Weissman, Dick – *Blues, The Basics* – Routledge Taylor & Francis Group 2005. ISBN 0415970687.

Videotapes
    The Land Where The Blues Began – Vestapol 13078
    Legends of Country Blues – Vestapol 13003
    Big City Blues – Rhapsody Films
    Chicago Blues – Rhapsody Films
    Stevie Ray Vaughan – Live from Austin, Texas
                EVD 201816 9.

DVDs
  The Blues - A Musical Journey:
    - Feel Like Going Home (Martin Scorsese)
    - The Soul of a Man (Wim Wenders)
    - The Road to Memphis (Richard Pearce & Robert Kenner)
    - Warming by the Devils Fire (Charles Burnett)
    - Godfathers and Sons (Marc Levin)
    - Red, White & Blues (Mike Figgis)
    - Piano Blues (Clint Eastwood)

Websites

Alligator.com
Allmusic.com
BBking.com
Blantonsbourbon.com
Bluesabout.com
Brown-forman.com
Buffalotrace.com
Elijahcraig.com
Fourroses.us
Guitar.about.com
Guitarmaker.com
Harmonicatunes.com
Heavenhill.com
Invention.smithsonian.org
Jackdaniels.com
Jimbeam.com
Johnleehooker.com

Keithrichards.com
Kokotaylor.com
Makersmark.com
Mountvernon.org
Muddywaters.com
Oldripvanwinkle.com
Robertjohnson
bluesfoundation.com
Rollingstones.com
Stevieray.com
Sugar-blue.com
Tommyshannon.com
Whiskeymuseum.com
Wikipedia.org
Wildturkeybourbon.com
Woodfordreserve.com

MEET THE BAND

Help Me
A Thank You Note with Willie Dixon & Rice Miller

In writing a book one needs support from friends and family, input and solace. The appropriate tune for me is the famous Willie Dixon song "Help Me," beautifully rendered by that great harmonica man Rice Miller, better known as Sonny Boy Williamson II.

I would like to thank the following people, who unknowingly formed an all-star band with which I could perform and write this book:

Woodye Bedford, Penryn Craig, Michael DeWitt, Lynne Grant, Bruce Iglauer, Larry Kass, Jack Kelley IV, Bonnie and Randall Lewis, David B. Lovett, Jack McCray, Jane Oxner Waring, David Pudlo, Candy Richards, Leon Rodenburg, Rini Roukema, Jimmy Russell, Jim Rutledge, Bill Samuels, Jr., David Scheurich, Steve Simon, George Stone, Angela Traver, Bas Van Der Groep, Marcel Van Gils, Julian Van Winkle, III, Klaas Vermeulen, Charles Waring III, Ronald Zwartepoorte and last but not least my dear wife and muse Becky Lovett Offringa.